Youth
Culture
Power

D1596111

Hip-Hop Education
Innovation, Inspiration, Elevation

Edmund Adjapong and Christopher Emdin
General Editors

Vol. 1

The Hip-Hop Education series is part of the Peter Lang Education list.
Every volume is peer reviewed and meets
the highest quality standards for content and production.

PETER LANG
New York • Bern • Berlin
Brussels • Vienna • Oxford • Warsaw

Jason D. Rawls and John Robinson

Youth
Culture
Power

A #HipHopEd Guide to Building
Teacher-Student Relationships
and Increasing Student Engagement

PETER LANG
New York • Bern • Berlin
Brussels • Vienna • Oxford • Warsaw

Library of Congress Control Number: 2019940688

Bibliographic information published by **Die Deutsche Nationalbibliothek**.
Die Deutsche Nationalbibliothek lists this publication in the "Deutsche
Nationalbibliografie"; detailed bibliographic data are available
on the Internet at http://dnb.d-nb.de/.

ISSN 2643-5551 (print)
ISSN 2643-556X (online)
ISBN 978-1-4331-7126-0 (hardcover)
ISSN 978-1-4331-7125-3 (paperback)
ISBN 978-1-4331-7127-7 (ebook pdf)
ISBN 978-1-4331-7128-4 (epub)
ISBN 978-1-4331-7129-1 (mobi)
DOI 10.3726/b15811

The paper in this book meets the guidelines for permanence and durability
of the Committee on Production Guidelines for Book Longevity
of the Council of Library Resources.

© 2019 Peter Lang Publishing, Inc., New York
29 Broadway, 18th floor, New York, NY 10006
www.peterlang.com

All rights reserved.
Reprint or reproduction, even partially, in all forms such as microfilm,
xerography, microfiche, microcard, and offset strictly prohibited.

Printed in the United States of America

TABLE OF CONTENTS

FOREWORD

Christopher Emdin

While cultural relevance in its many diverse and essential iterations has rightfully become part of the lexicon in schools of education and teacher preparation programs across the globe, teaching that reflects the culture of many of the most marginalized youth still remains absent or invisible. After decades of tireless work in advocating for culture, there has been an adoption of the language of cultural relevance and an overall acceptance that it has some role in teaching and learning. Unfortunately, this "progress" has been at the expense of populations whose culture holds tenets that challenge the very structure of schools. We accept only cultures that align to the existing structures of schools and search for justifications for why those that do not directly align are problematic. Cultural relevance then becomes the identification of cultures that maintain existing power structures or that makes power wielders comfortable. In particular, educators have not done much work interrogating the complexities of urban youth culture and identify its misalignment with the organizational and pedagogical structures of schools and schooling as a deficiency rather than a critique or alternate way of looking at schools. I assert that urban youth culture is not against education or being educated. It has rules of engagement and/or ways of knowing and being that support knowledge accumulation and creation. However, it is concurrently fundamentally opposed to how knowledge is created, developed and transferred in traditional schools. In an era of linguistic allegiance to culturally relevant, responsive and sustaining pedagogies, educators operate with shared language but are divided on belief systems and practices even within a framework of relevance. This is why hip-hop culture and an understanding of its complexity is essential for culturally relevant educators. Hip-hop serves as the ultimate example of the complexities of culture. It has multiple signs and meanings which each require deconstruction and deep analysis. It teaches us to go beyond what we see because of all that lies right beneath its surface.

Not only is a consideration of hip-hop essential to claiming cultural relevance, one cannot engage in/with hip-hop culture without unearthing that it holds within it a number of models for both how to teach and what it means to teach. This is very different than teaching with artifacts or aspects of the elements of hip-hop culture. It is about a hip-hop philosophy of teaching, learning and engagement as separate from formal education, existing outside of traditional educational spaces, but possible to be used to reimagine schools. This is Hip-hop not for, or as a tool of education, but hip-hop AS education. To engage in hip-hop as education, one must identify if they are willing to engage with all of the culture. One cannot receive all that Jason Rawls and John Robinson have to offer in this text without accepting that the culture of hip-hop has as much value as (if not more value than) the culture of school. The work presupposes that school must align itself to and learn from hip-hop and not the other way around. This is a challenging perspective for educators that are deeply invested in an assimilationist perspective which expects that youth bend their cultures to the needs of school. An educator with the intentions to be culturally relevant who aligns with an assimilationist philosophy will enact violence on young people even with the use of hip-hop because a misuse of the culture or a rendering of a superficial aspect of their culture as the cultural anchor of the instruction will yield a defensive stance from the student.

Rawls and Robinson offer a response to the sophomoric critique of hip-hop in education that uses the negative themes in mainstream popular music as its anchor. It argues for the complexity of culture and a recognition that a negative lyric often comes out of societal conditions that induce a visceral response and guttural articulation that has truth value. Most importantly, the same culture that produces negative lyrics consistently critiques, responds to and reimagines them. Selected lyrics are not culture en masse and any attempt to simplify a complex culture to mainstream popular lyrics is disingenuous at best. It is for this reason that this work takes up the challenge it does and expresses a more complex way to engage stakeholders in education.

This book is being released with/as an album to move us further towards reflecting hip-hop culture and its complexity in academic work. It is as much a sonic work as it is a text and is as much a sharing of information on how to teach as it is a critique of education. Rawls and Robinson offer a simple sophistication that is emblematic of who they have been in hip-hop for the last two decades. This offering of the self in written and audio formats represents a new direction for hip-hop education scholarship. It is a symbol of what Rawls offered hip-hop culture with his music production and creating/naming of Jazz-hop and its genre bending blending of Jazz and Hip-hop. In much the same way, this work moves the field and the culture towards what it professes to be—a space for all to share who they are in an authentic way while privileging the voice of youth and where they are in relation to schools and schooling.

GLOSSARY OF TERMS

A-Alikes: Two people who have the same behavioral characteristics. Often times they have similar personality traits, demeanor, taste and aesthetic.

Add on to the Cipher: To contribute valuable information to a conversation or project. To bring more resources to any situation in order to more productively build something.

Audi 5000: Hip-hop term from the Golden era of hip-hop meaning "goodbye" or "I am leaving"

CRP: Culturally Relevant Pedagogy—first described by Gloria Ladson-Billings

Do the Knowledge: Doing research to discover your own answers about a topic

Freaking Your Sneakers: This is how one manipulates shoelaces, usually involving sneakers or gym shoes

Free Free: Slang term used to describe free and reduced lunch

Freestyle: To Improvise Rap sentences without a plan or writing it down. Rapping whatever comes to mind right on the spot in the moment.

HHBE: Hip-hop Based Education

Micro-wave Generation: reference to the idea that Generation Z expects everything to happen in a quick and equally responsive manner

Old School: A term used to describe anything that is from a past era or something from an earlier tradition

The Real: A description of any nouns' authenticity, as in The Real HIP HOP!

The Science: A term used to describe instructions on how to do something

Youth Culture Pedagogy: A pedagogical approach which uses student culture to create scenarios to facilitate learning

INTRODUCTION

The journey to complete this mission of a book on hip-hop education has been long and arduous. However, it originally just started out as an album. John and I both did not initially begin our careers in the field of education. Our paths crossed in the world of underground hip-hop in the late 90's. Our first album, *The 1960's Jazz Revolution Again,* was a project that was born out of our mutual respect for jazz music and jazz culture. With us both being hip-hop kids, we also wanted to infuse hip-hop into this project about jazz music. We both grew up as big fans of hip-hop artists who sampled jazz into their work. This influenced both of our careers. I had begun using the term "Jazz-Hop" to describe boom-bap hip-hop with jazz influences. So that is how we began describing our first album, *The 1960's Jazz Revolution Again.*

When creating that album, we studied both the music and culture to help immerse our creative pallets for an album which would be the true definition of Jazz-Hop. John and I had worked on several songs before, but this was our first album project. We wanted it to set a standard. While creating that album, our process for creativity involved phone discussions about jazz greats who influenced much of our music. As we created that album, most of it was done while we weren't in the same room. It was a good process and it worked for that album. As I said before, we had always discussed creating a second album, but knew we wanted it to be more significant and more connected to the importance of culture and society.

With this album, our creative process grew exponentially. Instead of a few phone conversations, we felt it prudent to build and work primarily in the physical. We wanted this album to be more hands on. We spent more time together in the library (both in Brooklyn, New York, and Columbus, Ohio). We spent more time, on the phone or on video chats conceptualizing this project. We had a weekly phone conversation on Sundays to discuss and develop ideas for the album and book. We also took our time in the recording studio, actually only recording the album while we were in the same space. With this album, we made sure we added more of what we felt was a secret weapon on the first album; a singer named Tiffany Paige. She added such an important aspect to the first album. We wanted her to be more involved with this one. So she became a part of our creative process.

In addition, we added a new dimension to this project. Our focus was to use the songs to speak about what was going on in our classrooms. Then we thought we could take it a step further. What would happen if we not only used the album to introduce, define and categorize our theoretical perspectives but wrote a book which could be used by educators worldwide? It got us excited! We had even more motivation for this second project! For instance, as John and Tiffany finished each verse and hook for a song on the album, John would send me the lyrics as a word document. I would get to work outlining and formatting the song he wrote into a chapter for the book. I would then send John a draft of that chapter, and he would add on to the cipher. The whole process to creating this book and album project became more organic.

As we began to share our ideas with Dr. Emery Petchauer and Dr. Christopher Emdin, the whole project began to just flow together. This team would help us make this book project come to fruition in a way that was beyond our wildest dreams. The book and the album both just flowed naturally as the pair shared insight into this world of academia. Once we were able to share our ideas with members of the American Education Research Association Hip-Hop Sig, we were able to put the final pieces to this puzzle together. Consultation with these folks helped us shape and mold our ideas.

Our aim is to push forward the notion of using Hip-Hop Based Education (HHBE) to address issues of student engagement and teacher-student relationships using relational pedagogy and care. Additionally, this book seeks to expand the current theories of culturally relevant pedagogy and reality pedagogy. We will introduce you to our philosophy on education that we call

Youth Culture Pedagogy (YCP). We also want to introduce you to the embodiment of YCP that we call the C.A.R.E. model. We hope this book will open the door to more conversations in order to advance this burgeoning notion of using hip-hop and possibly even youth culture as a catalyst for change in the American education system. We designed this book and album to speak to teachers, administrators and parents who are part of the hip-hop generation. We want to establish a foundation of thought which speaks to the issue of connecting with students in a meaningful way based on the culture in which they engage.

With respect to the albums, we also recognize that the contemporary hip-hop of today's generation is vastly different from many of today's hip-hop educators (Rawls & Petchauer, 2019). So rather than try to make hip-hop music for today's generation of students, we decided to focus on reaching our generation of hip-hop heads, who are generally the educators. Since the book and the album are designed to go together, we expect to touch on many different learning styles. Some will discover our ideas from the book and hopefully our references to the album will make them curious enough to want to hear the album. We also realize that some, if not most of you, will find out about our theories from hearing the album first. Regardless of how you find the information, we hope you are inclined to delve into the other medium. Whether you enjoy reading to learn information or would rather enjoy listening to a hip-hop album, both are purposefully designed to enhance your learning.

While this project started out as just an album, the ideas and concepts were so vast, we felt they warranted a thorough analysis. It led us to work on both the album and the book simultaneously. However, we believe both can stand on their own. Our hope with the album is to spark an educational revolution similar to the revolution which was sparked in us when Public Enemy dropped "It Takes a Nation of Millions to Hold Us Back." Before that album, I had not yet heard of Malcolm X, Huey Newton or Louis Farrakhan. That album sparked my interest in these leaders. It made me curious about their messages. I had to do the knowledge. We hope this album will spark the same interest in educators and parents. We want to introduce or re-introduce them to great thinkers such as Paulo Freire, Asa Hillard and Gloria Ladson-Billings. We hope to push forward the teachings of some of our current #HipHopEd scholars such as Chris, Emery, P. Thandi Hicks Harper, Joycelyn Wilson, Bettina Love, James "The Fresh Professor" Miles, Martha Diaz, Timothy Davis, Sam Seidel, Edmund Adjapong, Amil Cook and Ian Levy. We want this album to spark interest for people to do the knowledge on their ideas and principles.

Another goal with this book is to revolutionize the PD (Professional Development) for teachers. We aim to dive deeper into the concepts introduced on the album and give a new voice to educators who want to revolutionize education. In its current format, professional developments for educators are dry and filled with details that may or may not be relevant to what one is teaching. We have attended many PD's in which we watch the teachers become the students they teach on a daily basis. Administrators or whoever is running the PD are often heard telling the teachers to "put your phones away." Teachers can be seen drifting off or randomly doodling, rather than paying attention to the speaker. We envision a livelier PD with performances, hand clapping and crowd participation; basically like one of our live performances. When we share our ideas with you, our intent is to have you up on your feet; energized, inspired and excited.

Our PD's are designed to be full of life. They are designed to be presented in a different way. We are performers. We rap. We DJ. We make beats. We believe in crowd participation. You will be encouraged to get out your seat and participate. It's the same philosophy that we bring to our classroom. We want you to use this book to bring excitement back to your classroom. Remember what it was like when you were sitting in those chairs. Remember what it was like at your last PD. Our aim is to make you rethink your teaching practice. The best way to explain how to do this is to show you.

One way we chose to ensure the book coincides with the album was to have each song title on the album match a chapter in the book. To strengthen the connection between the book and the album, we begin each chapter with a lyric from the song. The book is organized in such a way as to break down our thoughts and ideas into easy to follow sections. We wanted to model congruency as well so each chapter is set up in the exact same manner to make it easy to find what you are looking for in the chapter. Each section within each chapter is named for a term that shares its origins from Hip-Hop/Black/African-American discourse.

The first section for each chapter is called **"Say What."** This section is basically an introduction to the chapter and will give a brief description of the problem and why we chose to address that problem. The next section is called **"What's the Deal."** In this section, we dig deeper into some of the facts of the issue at hand in addition to our thoughts on how this issue affects students. In the **"What's the Science"** section, we give our solution to the problem using principles from YCP. Our aim in this section is to give you some insight into our thought processes and how we feel that YCP can be effective in some of these different situations.

The **"MC Notes"** section of each chapter will include John's thoughts and ideas which brought him to write each song on the album. This part of the book is very special to us because this is where we give insight into some of our logic and reasoning that inspired the album in addition to the book. Indeed, this section is how we connect the book to the album. We present these MC Notes as a case study of John's work as a teaching artist in the New York City public school system. It is where we see John's reflection on his direct experience using our methods. This section will be written in a less academic fashion and will be written in a more straightforward manner to give you "the real" of everyday issues encountered while teaching in an urban public school. Additionally, with the MC Notes section, our intention is to give you both the theoretical perspective of our concepts and to give you a practical perspective. The final section of each chapter is called **"Audi 5000."** This is the conclusion of each chapter in which you will find discussions and our final thoughts. We will also use this section to tie both our theoretical and practical perspectives.

Activities and ideas for classroom practice will be included in a separate **YCP Activity Guide** to accompany this book available as a pdf via our website www.itsjayare.com. This guide will include practical applications and examples of relationship building from our own classroom experiences. Also in this guide, you will find ideas that you can implement in your own classroom. These ideas can be used, changed, added to or subtracted from to fit the needs of your classroom.

References

Rawls, J. D. & Petchauer, E. (2019). *Be current, or you become the old man: Crossing the generational divide in hip-hop education.* Manuscript submitted for publication.

· 1 ·

YCP (YOUTH CULTURE POWER)

"We don't even gotta speak ... and we do the same things ... we stay connected world-wide ... we all know the same slang ... already changed the whole game"

Say What?

As we were researching and writing this book, the newest phenomenon to take place in our schools were Fidget Spinners. The Fidget Spinner was originally designed for students who have attention disorders or high anxiety to help them remain calm and focused. For some reason around the spring of 2017, they became the hottest toy on the market. John and I noticed that not only younger children were playing with them, but so were our high school students. It amazed us how quickly the phenomenon had taken place. My son even wanted one. While John teaches in Brooklyn, New York, I teach in Columbus, Ohio and we both noticed that students had the spinners almost around the same time. We spoke with other educators we knew around the country and the spinners were all over. Even my local news station did a TV report on them. We even noticed they were a part of youth culture across the globe (Rutherford, 2017). They were everywhere. And then, almost as fast as they had arrived on the scene, they were gone. They had been replaced by something else, and of course soon that new item would be replaced as well.

When the worldwide Fidget Spinner phenomenon was at its peak, we also noticed that schools were quick to ban them. We saw teachers taking spinners if students had them in class. This decision perplexed us both. We looked at this a bit differently than many of the administrators and teachers in our schools. We wondered about the cultural ramifications of these spinners. How did this thing become such a huge phenomenon in such a short period of time? How did kids all over the country and indeed, the world, find out about, get hooked, and then STOP using these things around or about the same time? Students were all on the same page with these toys. They saw them as a toy for right now. It was fun. It was engaging. The most important characteristic that we noticed is that they all knew. Teachers were not on the same page. The majority of us were behind the eight ball on this phenomenon and before we could notice what was going on, fidget spinners were old news.

When this happened, we reflected on our careers in education. We remembered other occasions when students picked up on something, got on board and were finished with something all before teachers and schools even picked up on the phenomenon. From flipping the water bottle in the water bottle challenge to loom bands, we noticed that this was a trend that occurred quite often. For me personally, one of the earliest of such trends was the onset of Twitter. I remember being in class and having one of my 8th grade students show me this new app in which I could write 140 characters of my own personal thoughts and anyone in the world could comment on it within seconds. My students were the first to show me this! I remember speaking to my good friend, DJ Rhettmatic and remember him telling me that I needed to get on this format to help promote my music. By the time many of us Generation X'ers caught on to this phenomenon, the youth of Gen Y and Gen Z had already stopped using Twitter as their primary communication app. And as with most new things, adults have now taken over as Twitter is most often mentioned in conjunction with politicians. Kids have moved on to other apps such as Snapchat. As John and I reflected on instances such as these, we begin to gain insight on what we felt was really happening in education today. This helped us to narrow our focus on our approach at pedagogical practice.

We believe this is around the time that we envisioned approaching education from the standpoint of youth culture. We began to understand that youth culture is at most times unspoken but still very influential. They don't even need to say words sometimes but they are all on the same page. The chorus to the song for this chapter says in part "We don't even gotta speak …

and we do the same things … we stay connected worldwide … we all know the same slang … already changed the whole game." In our minds, this is an important, often overlooked detail. How do they do this? How connected is it to popular culture? What can educators learn from this? It seemed to us that through technology and social media, they are all decisively linked and for the most part, all move in the same manner. We found it imperative to make it a priority to understand their culture to help us better understand their world, subsequently, allowing us to better educate them.

This chapter is our salute to youth culture. We will discuss the history of research behind it and also jump into our ideas about using youth culture as part of pedagogy. We will discuss the theories that helped us frame our ideas about youth culture as pedagogy. Subsequently, we will define YCP and explain the tenets intended to assist teachers with implementing it in the classroom. We will use the subsequent chapters to go into more depth about these tenets and to help further elaborate our thoughts on the role of youth culture in education.

What's the Deal?

I remember in 1995 or 1996, Talib Kweli (before he was signed) started one of his songs explaining that "all the great movements in history started with the youth …" This always stuck with me. The youth movement is powerful and generally a catalyst for change. The concept of youth culture first came into prominence around the turn of the century. Much of the research has been conducted in the United Kingdom. One thing we noticed during our research is that it can often times be paired with youth subculture or youth resistance (Shildrick, 2006; Tuck & Yang, 2014). All refer to the tendency of youth to be rebellious and have their own ways of doing, acting and living. Shildrick (2006) defined youth subculture as a subset or social group that acted differently than the dominant culture. Janssen, Deschesne and Van Knippenberg (1999) explained that there were two major lines of thinking to describe youth subculture, an aesthetic and empirical approach. The aesthetic approach is critical of the commercialized leisurely activities of young people. Many of these studies were done as just observation and without speaking to the young people. Conversely, the empirical approach to understanding youth culture focuses on positives and benefits that can be gleaned from young people. It settles on a more ethnographic form of data collecting and allows young people to express themselves.

For the last several years, scholars have advanced that an understanding of youth culture as part of pedagogy, specifically in the area of literacy, could be beneficial to student learning (Duncan-Andrade, 2004; Giroux, 2016; Mahiri, 2006; Morrell, 2002; Sandlin & Milan, 2008). Through paying attention to how youth express themselves through dress, music, activities even down to what apps they use can give teachers insight to help them become better readers (Janssen et al., 1999). Advancing ideas on hip-hop literacy, Mahiri (2001) assesses that teaching tools and methods have not advanced with the times. He suggests a method of what he calls "popular culture pedagogy" (Mahiri, 2001).

The idea of using popular culture as pedagogy is a concept that has been gaining popularity (Duncan-Andrade, 2004; Mahiri, 2006; Mojab & Taber, 2015; Morrell, 2002). The emphasis of this approach focuses on using mass media and its modes of transmission (television, video games, internet, movies etc.) as prompts for pedagogy. He adds that using these modes of transmission to teach offers educators a chance to reach students at a "multimodal, multitextual … multicultural" level, thereby allowing young people to conquer limits on learning and meaning because of the familiarity (Mahiri, 2001, p. 382). Gardner and Davis (2013) advance this notion, adding computer/mobile phone applications as an added mode of transmission. Janssen et al. (1999) affirm that mass media has had an effect on youth on a global scale and offers this as evidence as to why this form of pedagogy may be successful to help with literacy. Duncan-Andrade and Morrell (2008) further advanced these ideas by suggesting that teachers focus on adding hip-hop lyrics to aid in not only popular culture pedagogy but also in meeting students at their own level. Some teachers began to use Hip-Hop in the areas of literacy and English Language Arts. Petchauer (2015) labeled these early additions of hip-hop into pedagogy as the first wave of HHBE.

Scholars have termed this idea of meeting students at their level as critical pedagogy (Duncan-Andrade & Morrell, 2008; Emdin, 2009; McLaren, 1989). Meeting students at their level is defined as teachers working to enhance a students' current knowledge, using prior knowledge that students may already have. Stoval (2006) takes this concept a step further noting that critical should denote the active participation of both students and teachers. Both parties should actively work to learn and educate one another in the classroom. One possible way to employ this technique is tapping into a popular culture in which most students are involved (Emdin, 2009; Morrell, 2002). Morrell (2002) insists that educators pull elements from popular culture in order to reach students on a critical pedagogical level. Building from the ideology of McLaren (1989), Morrell (2002) theorizes using elements of popular culture as a catalyst to promote development in urban youth. The importance of reaching these students has been stressed in academia for quite some time. Freire (2007), Giroux (1989) and later McLaren (1989) theorized that critical pedagogy was important for students to develop a social justice stance and a consciousness of freedom.

The work of Gee (2003) also supports the idea of using popular culture, to inform the way that teachers educate. Gee (2003) declares that Discourse among social groups involving behavior, fashion, and perspectives among other characteristics, can lead to further understanding when working with students. Using literacy, he lays out tenets that characterize how learning is not a separate function of our lives and how students learn. Gee (2003) theorizes that (1) learning can occur both in formal and informal contexts, (2) learning is a social process, and finally, learning is grounded in historical precedence that shapes our ideas. These tenets directly align to meeting students at their level. They also support the idea that teachers should find out about their students' interests and experiences in order to become more effective teachers (Compton-Lilly, 2007; Gee, 2003). Thus, using popular culture as a means to tap into what students already know, and link it into something that they need to know, could possibly increase student engagement and learning outcomes (Christenson, Reschly & Wylie, 2012).

Scholars have successfully transferred these ideas to hip-hop literacy with studies on how the modes of transmission assist young people with constructing their identities (Dimitriadis, 2001; Morrell & Duncan-Andrade, 2002). Dimitriadis (2001) refers to Paul Willis's "common culture that young people create and sustain" (p. 30). This idea of youth having a common culture is exhibited in their fashion, creative consumption, hairstyles and overall identity (Willis, 2002). Willis (2002) goes on to describe common culture as a manifestation of how young people change the world around them to match their own interpretations. Dimitriadis (2001) adds that only by understanding these modes and themes of common culture can we understand young people and figure out how to work with them. With these ideas in mind, it seems to us that it only makes sense that we as educators should make an attempt to understand the common culture of young people.

What's the Science?

So what's the science? The science is applying pedagogy of youth culture. We feel that applying ideas brought forth in popular culture pedagogy and common culture gives legs to our movement of using YCP. These theoretical perspectives supported our ideas that we gleaned from the fidget spinner phenomenon. Subsequently, we felt that we could add on to these ideas based on our own previous experiences.

When formulating our approach to education, we believe that relationships and care are most important in the classroom. The student voice is also a valuable asset for a classroom teacher. In our own classroom experiences, we try to keep in mind the importance of building from what students already know. We feel that trying to advance their knowledge without acceptance of their prior knowledge is a fundamental flaw of the current education system. We also believe that one should educate students using methods that make sense to one's students. Moreover, a teacher should have the freedom to build relationships with her students and use these relationships to help shape curriculum. It is no secret that today's youth have their own culture. They move to the beat of their own drum. These youth have similar beliefs and values, which are heavily influenced by popular culture. Moreover, in many instances, these groups have similar characteristics based on geographic area, class, or socio-economic status. As previously mentioned, numerous scholars have studied the phenomenon of youth culture, subculture and resistance (Blackman, 2005; Blackman, 2014; Porfilio & Carr, 2010; Shildrick, 2006; Tuck & Yang, 2014). However, we intend to focus our efforts on the beliefs, values, characteristics and behaviors of marginalized urban students.

Our thoughts on youth culture align with Dr. P. Thandi Harper Hicks's understanding of youth popular culture and how hip-hop has influenced it. Hicks Harper (2000) defines youth popular culture "as that which is 'in', contemporary, and has the stamp of approval of young people (p. 2). One of the most important distinctions that she makes is that youth popular culture transcends boundaries of race, geographical boundaries and socio-economic status. With these ideals in mind, we think it is imperative for teachers to at least have a working knowledge of this culture. It seems that it would be nearly impossible to effectively communicate with one's students without having an understanding of what "engulfs and contextualizes" their lives (Hicks Harper, 2000, p. 1).

We call our approach to education, Youth Culture Pedagogy (YCP). This book will lay the groundwork for YCP and how we envision its use within the classroom. YCP is rooted in a foundation of culturally relevant pedagogy (Ladson-Billings, 1995a), reality pedagogy (Emdin, 2016) and Hip-Hop Based Education (Hill, 2009; Hill & Petchauer, 2015). We define YCP as a pedagogical approach which uses student culture to create scenarios to facilitate learning. Because we believe that YCP must be embedded with characteristics of relational pedagogy (Sidorkin, 2002) and an ethic of care (Noddings, 2002), our explanation of it will be saturated within these models. Subsequent chapters of this book will be dedicated to painting YCP in the light of these theoretical platforms. In addition, we have created four tenets that teachers can adopt in order to practice YCP in their classrooms. These four tenets state that teachers should embrace youth culture, create an affable learning environment for students, build and maintain positive relationships with students and develop an egalitarian teaching style which allows students to be themselves in the classroom. We will go more in depth on these tenets later in this chapter.

Now that we have given you our definition of YCP, let us expound on what we feel are the roots of our theoretical perspective, outline our tenets to facilitate implementation, and finally, suggest why we feel it would work in the classroom.

The Roots of Youth Culture Pedagogy

When framing our pedagogical praxis, we were influenced by the concept that young people follow a common culture. We would often try out ideas using pedagogy based on popular culture and have successes in our classrooms. Students seemed to enjoy when the teacher brought things they understood into the classroom. We would often incorporate concepts and ideas from several scholars to try out in our classroom. But the ideas that seemed to work best for us was Ladson-Billings (1995a) CRP, Emdin's (2016) reality pedagogy, and, of course relevant ideology from HHBE (Hill, 2009; Hill & Petchauer, 2015). In the following paragraphs, we will define each of these theories and then explain how we used them to devise our own philosophies.

Culturally Relevant Pedagogy (CRP)

Culturally Relevant Pedagogy, as first described by Ladson-Billings (1995b) has become one of the most common approaches to teaching. As such, several extensions of her original idea, such as culturally responsive or sustained pedagogies, have become common teaching practices as well. We felt it prudent to speak about these extensions and discuss their differences. When it comes to culturally relevant, responsive or sustained pedagogy, sometimes these terms may be used interchangeably. We want to clearly denote how we define each term based on our research. We define culturally relevant pedagogy (CRP) as an approach to teaching that considers the unique cultural backgrounds of youth (Ladson-Billings, 1995a). Ladson-Billings further explains CRP as being "connected to students, their families, their communities and their daily lives" (Ladson-Billings, 2014, p. 74).

Similar to CRP, culturally responsive teaching is based on the premise that students' perform better in school when academics and policies are based on student culture (Gay, 2000). While many scholars have defined the idea of responsive pedagogy, we define culturally responsive pedagogy as a focus on teachers' acceptance of their own specific cultural heritage and that of the school and curriculum as it relates to the culture of their students (Delpit, 1995; Emdin, 2009; Emdin, 2011a). Emdin (2011a) further elaborates that teachers are more effective when "they know how to deliver content in a way that resonates with their students and causes (them) to take ownership of the content and explore it more deeply on their own" (p. 285). Later, Paris (2012) hypothesized an idea of Culturally Sustained Pedagogy (CSP). He defined this as a "teachers need to meaningfully value and maintain the practices of extending their students' repertoires of practice to include dominant language, literacies, and other cultural practices" (Paris, 2012, p. 95).

Culturally sustained pedagogy (CSP) is the next stage of development for culturally relevant pedagogy (Paris, 2012). Paris (2012) defines CSP as pedagogy that "perpetuates and fosters linguistic, literate and cultural pluralism as part of the democratic project of schooling" (p. 93). Ladson-Billings (2014) suggests that CSP is CRP in practice and is necessary for student growth. We believe that in order to practice any type of sustaining pedagogy, one must keep youth culture in mind. Ladson-Billings (2014) agrees stating that it is imperative that we keep youth culture in mind when discussing sustained or relevant pedagogy (Ladson-Billings, 2014). She further explains that culture is ever changing and as educators, we must be able to adjust and keep up with these changes.

Ladson-Billings concept of keeping youth culture in mind when striving toward culturally relevant pedagogy aligns with the tenets of YCP. First, by embracing youth culture, a teacher demonstrates a commitment to connecting with students in their daily lives, communities and families. Second, teachers who care enough to create an affable learning environment and developing an egalitarian teaching environment demonstrate a willingness to work to sustain a sense of cultural awareness in the classroom. Part of the success of creating this CRP model is working toward trying to maintain it over a period of time. Finally, teachers who build and maintain relationships with students embody Ladson-Billings (1995b) culturally relevant pedagogy because they inherently are working toward understanding the student for who they are as a person.

Reality Pedagogy

It's no secret that we are heavily influenced by Dr. Christopher Emdin and his work in urban science education. We were fortunate enough to collaborate with him for this project. One of his ideas that shed light on our path was his theory of reality pedagogy and the acknowledgement of students' cultural capital. Adjapong and Emdin (2015) describe cultural capital as the value (or capital) that students bring into the classroom based on their own culture. Emdin (2009) expresses the benefits of using hip-hop culture and embracing this understanding, or cultural capital, through his explanation of transactional levels in the classroom. Emdin believes that a transaction (an exchange of information) and not just an interaction (in which only one party receives information) should occur in the classroom (Elon University, 2012). This way, the teacher demonstrates that she not only values students' culture but also values information and ideas students bring from prior experiences.

With respects to reality pedagogy, Emdin (2016) declares that teachers should empower students and value the cultural capital they bring to the table. Moreover, in alignment with Ladson-Billings (1995b) and the CRP model, he posits that the highest level of learning occurs when students are actively involved in all aspects of classroom functions including the creation of lesson plans and implementation of procedures (Emdin, 2009). Emdin (2009) labels this approach as reality pedagogy. He defines it as "moving beyond efforts to address the challenges within urban schools that focus on the academic deficiencies of youth to instead support both teachers and their students in improving their classroom experiences" (Emdin, 2009, p. 9). With the implementation of such an approach, the benefits for students include empowerment, voice, self-efficacy, and the creation of a community of learners (Ladson-Billings, 1995b; Milner, 2011; Petchauer, 2011; Wallaert & Wessell, 2011).

Emdin (2011b) strengthens his explanation with his 5 C's of reality pedagogy. First, he speaks about *co-generative* dialogues which are structured dialogues that build on students' hip-hop sensibilities. Second, Emdin (2011b) uses *co-teaching* as a way to allow students a chance to be experts at pedagogy (p. 288). Thereby, allowing students and teachers to learn from one another (creating a transaction rather than an interaction) in the classroom. Third, his approach to Appaiah's (2007) *cosmopolitanism* states that all human beings are responsible for one another (Emdin, 2011b). Therefore, the classroom should be treated no differently. Students and teachers should care for one another and differences should be valued. Fourth, Emdin (2011b) expresses the importance of *context* in allowing students to connect their home lives and culture with the classroom. Finally, he explains that *content* in the classroom "evolves out of the willingness of the teacher to acknowledge his or her own limitations" (Emdin, 2011b, p. 291). Thereby teachers give up some authority, allowing student voice to be prominent within the classroom setting.

Through an understanding of students' cultural capital and these 5 C's, we can see how YCP begins to form. YCP inherently values students' cultural capital. Just by embracing youth culture, a teacher demonstrates that she is not only interested in students' cultural capital but relies on it to inform her decisions, policies and even lesson plans. By creating a pleasant learning environment, the teacher drives Emdin's (2011b) ideals of co-teaching, context and Cosmopolitanism. While co-generative dialogues and content align seamlessly with a classroom that follows YCP's egalitarian teaching format. The idea of building and maintaining relationships mesh well with Emdin's reality pedagogy because YCP places importance on the students' cultural capital.

Hip-hop Based Education (HHBE)

As our primary experiences have been in the classrooms of urban schools, and because we consider ourselves part of the hip-hop generation, we will focus our efforts through Hip-Hop Based Education (HHBE). In our schools, hip-hop culture is a dominant culture within the classroom. While we do admit that hip-hop is not the only culture that many youth relate to, we feel it is widespread enough to speak to many marginalized youth. According to *Forbes*, Nielsen confirms that rap music has taken over as the most prevalent genre of music (McIntyre, 2017). *Sunday TODAY* with Willie Geist reports that Rap and R&B combined make up 40% of the Billboard Top 100 list compared to 25% ten years ago (Mania & Janiak, 2018). With this in mind, we believe that hip-hop culture could be useful in building relationships and conveying care with students. We believe that one should use hip-hop aesthetics and practices in an effort to move toward hip hop theory and to assist teachers in making stronger connections to students real lived experiences (Hill & Petchauer, 2015).

In order to go in depth about HHBE, we must first take a step back and have a brief discussion about hip-hop and the culture created around it. Born in the Bronx in the early 1970's, hip-hop was created by DJ's who only had turntables and records. Many of them could not afford instruments to "create" music. They had to think of new and innovative ways to create music. They did this by finding the "breakbeat" (or solo drum break of the song) and using two of those records on two turntables to extend that beat for the B-Boys and B-Girls to dance to. The dancing to these breakbeats eventually became known by the mainstream as breakdancing. Coupled with graffiti and later emceeing (or rhythmically rhyming over these breakbeats) these would eventually be known as the four elements of hip-hop (DJing, B-Boying or Breakdancing, Graffiti, MCing). The behavior and norms that became associated with these four elements (and later several others that have been added such as knowledge and beatboxing) form the culture of hip-hop. Although it has grown and changed, this culture still thrives to this day. This is the culture on which HHBE is based.

As mentioned previously, the first wave of HHBE concentrated on using rap lyrics in the classroom as part English Language Arts (Dimitriadis, 2001; Morrell & Duncan-Andrade, 2002; Petchauer, 2015; Stovall, 2006). Scholars are now advancing the use of hip-hop culture and aesthetics in the classroom to reach more marginalized students (Emdin, 2016; Hill & Petchauer, 2015; Petchauer, 2015). In the last few years, scholars have pushed toward a trend of not just analyzing but actually using various modes of production hip-hop in pedagogy, such as women's studies and the sciences. Petchauer (2015) has labeled this new school of HHBE as the "second wave" of HHBE.

In the last two decades, HHBE has become extremely popular as a form of Ladson-Billings's (1995a) CRP. Originally used as content in classrooms to reach marginalized youth, the influence of HHBE has grown as the popularity of hip-hop music has become popular worldwide (Hill, 2009). HHBE has permeated the curriculum at the middle, secondary and collegiate levels of education (Chang, 2005; Emdin, 2009; Irizarry, 2009; Petchauer, 2009; Rodriguez, 2009; Stovall, 2006). In the "first wave" of HHBE, as educators began incorporating hip-hop into their pedagogy, many of them used rap lyrics to help engage students in English and Language Arts course work. During this time, hip-hop lyrics were mostly used to develop critical literacy skills (Hill, 2009; Duncan-Andrade & Morrell, 2008) and as text for language classes (Alim, 2007). Reading supplements to aid student learning, such as the Hip-Hop Educational Literacy Program (H.E.L.P.) by Gabriel "Asheru" Benn (Benn, n.d.) and Flocabulary (Beninghoff, 2006) became popular methods of engagement in the classroom. In her dissertation, Hall (2007) insists that hip-hop has an engaging "crossover appeal" with students (p. 38). This cross-over appeal refers to the certain aspects of hip-hop culture that are desirable to some youth such as music, rapping and fashion. Hip-hop resonates with many youth and there has been a push to use its appeal to engage them in other aspects of their lives (Petchauer, 2012). Petchauer (2012) explains that initially there were three aspects of HHBE that a teacher could use to add to educational processes. These three aspects are as follows:

- Using hip-hop lyrics as an educational tool to teach academic content
- Studying hip-hop as a legitimate text in and of itself
- Using habits of body and mind inherent in hip-hop education

As mentioned previously, it is important to point out that HHBE has been vastly associated with CRP for quite some time (Hollie, n.d.; Irby, 2015). More recently, scholars have made a call for a more sustained use of HHBE in elementary and middle school education, women's and queer studies (Ladson-Billings, 2014; Lindsey, 2015; Love, 2015; Paris, 2012; Veel & Bredhauer, 2009; White, 2009; Young, 2010).

As HHBE has evolved, a new shift is occurring in the use of Hip-Hop in classrooms. The idea of using Hip-Hop culture in the classroom to shape class-room environment, strategies and policy has been termed the "second wave" of HHBE (Petchauer, 2015, p. 97). According to Petchauer (2015), the 'second wave' of HHBE should involve an aesthetic approach to practice and a more ethnographic approach to research. He clarifies that the culturally relevant pedagogy that embodied the first wave of HHBE was not "misguided" but "a natural progression" toward growth of the field (Petchauer, 2015, p. 97).

Part of this approach involves using the many nuances within hip-hop that guide and influence the culture. In many instances, teachers are not given the adequate training, resources or realistic time frame to achieve many of the goals set for them. Yet, they are still held by a standard that expects them to accomplish these goals and beyond. How can teachers achieve these lofty goals with limited resources? This is where HHBE comes into play. Similar to the origins of Hip-Hop music, HHBE calls on teachers to make something out of nothing. Going back almost 100 years, Dewey emphasizes the importance of developing student's critical thinking skills by encouraging further inquiry of students. Further, Freire (1970) and later, Ladson-Billings (1995b) insists that educators should even present material in ways that allow students to make connections with their own lives.

It is within this "second wave" of HHBE, which we feel our ideas align. Petchauer (2015) lays out how the aesthetic forms of HHBE could be instrumental in "harnessing abstract concepts from hip-hop expressions and applying them in specific educational settings" (Petchauer, 2015, p. 99). He explains how the classroom is similar to major Hip-Hop idiosyncrasies such as sampling & layering, flow & rupture, and performance & embodiment. In Hip-Hop music, beat makers sample notes and sounds from another source and proceed to chop and layer it to create new soundscapes. In this same sense, teachers can sample bits and pieces of information from old and new sources to layer new frameworks in which students can learn (Petchauer, 2010; Petchauer, 2015). While flow in Hip-Hop culture exemplifies aesthetics such as rapping, graffiti, B-Boying (dancing) and DJing (the four elements of Hip-Hop); flow can be defined in the classroom as normal everyday processes. These processes can include the rupture or disruption of those processes in the classroom that are comparable to the breaks in flow in all of the elements of Hip-Hop (i.e. The break in a DJ's beat juggling routine or the break in a dance routine for a B-Boy). These are changes to the routine that take place and allow progression to happen. As Petchauer (2015) explains, there must be flow before rupture can take place. In Hip-Hop, "catching wreck," means to achieve respect or receive accolades for a job well done. This means that, as in Hip-Hop, rupture (or wreck) is a natural break in flow and when it occurs in the classroom; this wreck can be a positive or negative experience for both teachers and students. The "affective engagement, performance and embodiment of Hip-Hop" are all expressed as 'doing' something in Hip-Hop. In Hip-Hop culture, participants are all involved, and movement is almost always required (Petchauer, 2015, p. 86). The classroom, in this second wave of HHBE, should also resemble this same scenario; as students should be actively engaged and involved. This is how we envision our classroom with regards to YCP. Quite frankly, this is also how we envision a PD course for teachers.

As mentioned before, up until now, HHBE has been primarily used as an extension of culturally relevant pedagogy. Now, HHBE is developing its own theories that are guided by culturally aesthetic frameworks and ethnographic research (Dimitriadis, 2015; Irby, 2015; Petchauer, 2015). HHBE should be a foundation of theory and not just a subset of culturally relevant pedagogy. As such, Petchauer (2015) suggests that researchers use HHBE approaches for other aspects of the educational process. In fact, Emdin and Adjapong (2018) argue "for a philosophical and conceptual understanding of hip-hop as education" (p. 3). The Fresh Prep program in New York City is an example of this process. The program is designed to draw on students' cultural tendencies to engage high school seniors at risk of not graduating (Cherfas, Casciano & Wiggins, 2018). It uses hip-hop and youth culture to re-conceptualize learning in order to pass the state test. Examples such as this elicit new directions in exploring different learning styles and multiple learning intelligences through HHBE (Gardner, 2011). Thus we are at a time when hip-hop can be used to assist scholars with creating theoretical constructs. It's time to revolutionize how we educate.

YCP is designed to be a part of this revolution. YCP is a practical based application that was born from the perspective of various educators experiences. In this line of pedagogical discourse, teachers use untraditional means to build relationships and express care. YCP says embracing youth culture is imperative and in HHBE, lessons are built around students' own culture. Instead of forcing students to give up the things they frequent, we feel teachers should discuss them and when possible, use them in lessons, thus creating an affable learning environment through an egalitarian teaching style. All of these characteristics are important when building and maintaining relationships with students.

We have given you some insight into YCP. But the real question we would like to answer right now is, "How can I implement YCP?" The last few sections have discussed how our ideas were informed by other scholars and theories. These are ideas we have been reading about and studying for years. We have practiced these ideas in our own classrooms but always realized that all of these ideas circled back to one important aspect of teaching. Quite frankly, it all boils down to caring for students. Keep this in mind as you read the next section.

The 4 Tenets of Youth Culture Pedagogy

In order to enact YCP, there are several characteristics teachers must exhibit. With a goal of empowering students, giving them a voice and imparting a sense of community, we developed 4 major attributes to which a classroom teacher should strive. As mentioned before they are as follows:

1. Teachers should embrace youth culture
2. Teachers should create an affable learning environment
3. Teachers should build and maintain positive relationships with students
4. Teachers should aim to develop an egalitarian teaching style

Culture

In this book, we have already spoken about and will continue to speak about culture to varying degrees. Culture is defined as a way of life shared by people in a place or time (Culture, n.d.). Culture is such a broad term and, in education, is often related to studying the ways of our students' lives. We use it in a similar fashion as Ladson-Billings and Emdin since we believe that it's important to understand our students' ways of life so that we can understand the best way to teach them. However, the following definition by Hilliard is the one we will use for our book. He explains "culture is nothing, more nor less, than the shared ways that groups of people have created to use and define their environment" (Hilliard, 2002, p. 89).

John Locke once described students as blank slates that need to be filled with curricular content. David Kirkland goes so far as to say that at this point we are even treating students as "dirty slates that need to be washed" (High Tech Slam, 2015). For years, teachers have tried to tailor schools today to fit the mode of how school was in their day. The problem with this thinking lies with one word; change. With the advent of new technologies and how fast paced society has become, this is not a plausible solution. Change is undeniable. Society in general has changed. Youth culture changes with each generation. The notion that students should just sit in a desk and be taught to is incredibly unrealistic in this day and age. The days of education based on students as blank tablets or empty vessels are far gone. Since this generation moves to the beat of their own drum, why not embrace this?

Embracing youth culture takes pressure off the teacher because instead of always saying "no", the teacher can ask youth to define why they do what they do. Teachers should have students explain why they have that Fidget Spinner. Tell them to describe why they enjoy trying to flip the bottle of water. By embracing youth culture, we mean teachers should be learning about the beliefs, values, characteristics and behaviors of this generation from their students.

As previously mentioned, a huge influence on our research was the work of Ladson-Billings. We wanted to expand on her work and use culture in a more meaningful way to impact student's lives. In our classrooms we noticed that often times, students had their own manner of being and doing. When we embraced this and showed an interest, we found much more success in our classroom. In fact, in later speeches, Ladson-Billings has said that she has been excited to see inquiries into CRP evolving into some new and exciting ways

(UMH Hurley Convergence Center, 2017). She also expressed that one of the shortcomings of some of her early work was not focusing on youth culture (UMH Hurley Convergence Center, 2017).

Affability

When discussing what it means to be affable, we feel the best description is a state of being pleasant. The dictionary defines affability as "easy to approach and talk to; warm, friendly and polite" (Affability, n.d.). While it may be unrealistic to expect a teacher to be all of these things every day for each class period, we think by simply creating an environment in which students perceive this affability can contribute to a caring classroom. Moreover, an affable classroom combined with empathy and care leads to a more sustaining education (Jensen, 2016; Noddings, 2005).

In a study based on understanding why students gravitate toward which teachers, the affability of the teacher was considered most relevant to building relationships and trust (Kim & Wei, 2011). Furthermore, the approachability of the teacher was generally considered to be one of the most important factors of positive interactions between student and teacher (Kim & Wei, 2011). In another study, Richmond (1990) found that creating an environment of compliance vs. motivation led to negative student behaviors. She found that most authoritative or coercive classroom settings led to behaviors that may have led to short-term compliance but the overall effect on student behavior was negative. These findings add to our ideas on the importance of affability in the classroom. Later, we will explain why YCP is based on building relationships and expressing care for students. Creating an affable learning environment supports this as well and is an important first step toward shifting archaic behavioral methods toward more culturally relevant methods. An affable learning environment is a product of caring relationships.

Relationships

When speaking about student engagement and outcome, some questions come to mind. Why are students more apt to trust some teachers rather than others? What makes a student confide in teacher A as opposed to teacher B? How is trust and harmony built in a relationship between teacher and student? How can I keep my students engaged and interested? These are questions that many teachers have possibly posed at some point in their career. While Hart, Stewart & Jimerson (2011) contend that student engagement is an important

concept connected to student success, Jones (2008) believes that "strong positive relationships are critical" to student engagement (p. 6). Scholars posit
that student learning outcomes and engagement are affected by far more than
just what happens in the classroom (Aspelin, 2011; Ladson-Billings, 1995a;
Mahiri, 2001). For instance, Gergen (2009) asserts that the relational aspect
of teaching is not only important for understanding student engagement, but
is the foundation for inspiring student performance.

We believe that strong positive relationships are at the core of what YCP
is all about. Without a strong relationship with students, teachers will have a
difficult time facilitating instruction. We have seen this time after time in our
schools. Teachers struggle with classroom management or engagement because
they haven't taken the time to build strong relationships with students. As a
classroom teacher, I had very few discipline issues. Most times, I was able to
speak to my students in a one-on-one setting and generally get to the root of
the behavior issue. However, this is not plausible if there is no relationship.
Teachers, who make connections with students early in the school year, will see
decreased behavior incidences later. Moreover, these connections are important not only to a student's ability to learn, but to a student's socialization.

Similar concepts have been discussed in numerous studies. For example,
Stuhlman and Pianta's (2001) study was designed to understand teacher-
student relationships by assessing narratives from teachers about those relationships. They found that (1) the teacher's narratives corresponded to the
observed behaviors of both teacher and student in the classroom, (2) teacher
narratives were consistent to previous methods studied about the teacher-
student relationship, and (3) teacher relationship narratives and child interactions support claims that there are emotional connections made within the
classroom. Sidorkin (2000) theorizes about relationships between teachers
and students, stating that building relationships with students should be a priority more so than monitoring behaviors in students. By focusing on building
relationships rather than the present state of student behavior, the teacher
promotes a growth opportunity for meaningful interaction. Noddings (2005)
hypothesized about the importance of relationships and caring as a goal and
fundamental aspect of education. Both Noddings (2002, 2005) and Sidorkin
(2002) concluded that caring relations should be the foundation for educators
as they build relationships with students in their classrooms.

Scholars have hypothesized on the importance of building relationships
with students (Baker, Grant & Morlock, 2008; Barile, Donohue, Anthony,
Baker, Weaver & Henrich, 2012; Clemmons, 2006; Frisby & Martin, 2010;

Frisby & Myers, 2008; Wilson, Ryan & Pugh, 2010). Students seem to be interested in the personal experiences of their instructors. They are engaged when instructors share these experiences and use them for classroom knowledge (Catt, Miller & Schallenkamp, 2007). According to Sull (2009), instructors should strive to have an "ongoing positive connection" to students in order to build relationships and ultimately contribute to student success (p. 93). Student interpersonal relationships with instructors have been studied with respect to various fields such as: teacher-student interaction in an elementary school (Doumen, Koomen, Buyse, Wouters & Verschueren, 2012; Pianta, 1999), teacher-voice and student connections (Clemmons, 2006), and professor-college student relationships (Catt et al., 2007; Frisby & Martin, 2010; Frisby & Myers, 2008; Wilson et al., 2010). Catt et al. (2007) also found that teachers who built interpersonal relationship were paramount in developing students who valued education and learning. Additionally, in their study, Frisby and Martin (2010) found that teacher-student relationships were a consistent predictor in participation, affective learning and cognitive learning. Similarly, Frisby and Myers (2008) found students' level of engagement and motivation was directly correlated to the teacher-student relationship. Lastly, in their study of teacher immediacy, Wilson et al. (2010) found that the teacher-student relationship was a predictor of student outcomes.

Fullan (2003) declares teachers must gain their students' trust. He further explains that trust is one of the most important elements in developing teacher-student relationships. Weiner (2003) describes trust as the "bedrock" of teacher-student relationships (p. 370). Additionally, Docan-Morgan (2009) suggests that trust helps define and allows these relationships. According to Noddings (2002), this trust can be a result of care exhibited by a teacher in the classroom. In order to build relationships with students, teachers should meet students at their level (Emdin, 2009). This coincides with being culturally relevant.

With regards to maintaining this cultural relevancy, we keep in mind, Emdin's description of getting a transaction in the classroom and not just an interaction (Elon University, 2012). One way to do this is to allow students to have more control in the classroom. The next section describes how we achieve this within YCP.

Egalitarian

Freire (1970) spoke of the importance of social change with his ideas about critical pedagogy. Generally, a classroom community can be run with several different structures. In some of classrooms, we have observed democracy, dictatorship. However, we think an egalitarian approach delineates our methods best. Merriam-Webster defines egalitarian as a belief in human equality with respect to social, political and economic affairs (Egalitarian, n.d.). Now let's be clear. Do we believe that students will be treated as equals with the same power as the teacher in the classroom? No. We do acknowledge that there is a power imbalance in the classroom. The teacher-student dynamic in the classroom is one that can easily fall into the "it's my classroom, do as I say" mode of thinking. True equality or mutuality in the classroom may be impossible to achieve (Rawls, 2017). However, the part of the definition we want to impress upon you the reader is that egalitarian is a "belief in human equality." Egalitarian thinking says that a person will respect other individual's ideas on social, political and economic affairs. One may not agree with those ideas, but they respect the other person's right to have these ideas. With a teaching style based on this belief, the teacher respects student's cultural capital. With this belief, YCP principles are possible. The path to this approach is in Sidorkin's (2000, 2002) relational pedagogy.

One of the leaders in the field of relational pedagogy is Sidorkin. Sidorkin (2000) believes "that education is a function of specific relations and not behaviors" (p. 1). He emphasizes that there must be a shift from a pedagogy of behavior to a pedagogy of relation. This concept will be an overarching theme of this book. Currently, behavior management is currently the most prevalent approach to classroom management. It is an approach we feel is archaic and stagnant. Sidorkin links relational ontology, as described by Biesta (2004) and Margonis (1999a, 1999b), to build a case for classifying relational pedagogy in a taxonomic light. Thus the term pedagogy of relation emerges and will be used in this book.

The majority of research in this field centers mostly on relationships at an interpersonal level. Its roots can be traced to Buber (1958) who explained relations in education with his I-Thou and I-It concept. Buber explains when the "I" relates to another human being, the "Thou" meets this "I." However, when the "I" relates to the world, the "It" meets the "I." In other words, a person reacts in a twofold way when met with distinct types of relational situations. The I-Thou is a mutual correlation between two human beings, while the I-It is an experience which connects how we personally experience, know and manage things around us. In this concept, participants immediately relate to one another or the relationship is mediated (Buber, 1958). With regards to education, Buber (2003) later believed that although mutuality is needed for

relational education, this was unable to be achieved due to the power imbalance in schools between teacher and student.

In order to describe pedagogy of relation, Sidorkin (2002) disputes Buber's
(2003) claim that true mutuality cannot exist in an I-Thou relationship
for teachers and students. Sidorkin (2002) explains that a different viewpoint must be taken in order to understand how mutuality can work in the
classroom. Teachers must pay attention to the relations in their classrooms
rather than behaviors. Similar to Gergen (2009) and Aspelin (2011), Sidorkin (2002) notes that "relations do not describe an individual; they always
describe a group or pair of people" (p. 1). Further, human relations always
contain a "component of emotion, attitude, past history and social context"
(Sidorkin, 2000, p. 3). Relations can change but they are always just there;
they never disappear. Similar to Noddings (2002), Sidorkin (2002) explains
that relations are usually associated with feminine qualities, such as feelings
or intuition, but this is not enough to really explain what relations are. Since
relations can only be described as being between two or more, Sidokin (2002)
uses the term polyphonic authority to underscore the idea that student voice
should be included in a classroom setting. He defines polyphonic authority
as the power that teachers share with students in the classroom as a way to
reconcile "the power imbalance with mutuality of relation" (Sidorkin, 2002,
p. 145). Sidorkin (2002) further advances that teachers must relinquish power
in the classroom in order to give students reason free participation and allow
the dialogical process to occur. Students must be included in the dialogue
about relations in schools in order to achieve true mutuality. More about the
importance of this dialogue among students and teachers follows.

To move from theory to practice with respects to polyphonic authority,
Sidorkin (2002) believes that we must include the student voice in all aspects
of the educational process. Claiming that most of the educational books written today are for the teachers, he even implies that a book be written to be
used by both teachers and students for educational practices. He sees this
polyphonic authority as a solution to the central problem of achieving true
mutuality in relational pedagogy. Sidorkin (2002) argues that dialogue in the
classroom is so important that it should be considered to be the core of human
existence, prompting that we cannot exist without it. Polyphonic authority
creates mutuality by allowing the student voice to be central in activities and
decision-making. In a later chapter, we will discuss how important this dia-
log with and between students can be to building relationships. In practice,
Sidorkin (2002) describes the teacher making the classroom a novel. In this

novel the teacher allows each student to share their stories and to learn from the stories of others in the class. In this respect, the teacher relinquishes her monophonic authority and is more of a guide as each student shares his or her story. We view the effort of a teacher to create this polyphonic authority as an egalitarian teaching style.

Freire (1970) suggests that all learning is relational. He argues that learning occurs due to interactions between people. Student experiences are the foundation for their own knowledge, and teachers who create a scenario such as the classroom as a novel allow students to share their voice. Yosso (2005) notes that valuing the views of socially marginalized individual's increases cultural capital within the classroom. As previously mentioned, Ladson-Billings (1994) first introduced her theory of culturally relevant (CRP) pedagogy by discussing the importance of teachers hearing the student voice. CRP aligns with relational pedagogy because it coincides with Sidorkin's (2002) approach to viewing the classroom as a novel. According to Catt et al. (2007) teachers cannot be effective without being able to communicate with students. Through building relations and effective communication, teachers can be able to guide positive development of the child. In order to guide them to academic success and global citizenship, we believe that a teacher should be able to relate to students through culture.

C.A.R.E

The primary words of our four tenets are Culture, Affability, Relationships and Egalitarian. If you look at the beginning of each word in our theory, you will see the true answer to using YCP in your classroom and striving toward being a successful teacher. Care is the most important aspect of being a teacher. Through concepts such as embracing youth culture, creating an affable learning environment, building and maintaining relationships and offering an egalitarian teaching style, teachers can display care to students. Most educators are most likely already doing some of even all of these things. However, YCP asks us to put them all together and use them to help make our classrooms a place where both the student and teacher get something out of the relationship.

As we said before, we believe that the profession of teaching is a calling. Due to the simple fact that it involves lives, feelings and interactions between at least two human beings, we feel that this is an altruistic profession that may not be for everyone. One must possess an innate disposition to want to help others. One of the most telling nuances of this profession is the students.

They can very easily discern the true nature of a teacher's heart and quickly determine if they genuinely care for them or not. Quite simply, if you are in in the profession for them, they will know it and make the job of the teacher that much more difficult. A teacher who is miserable in her job is even more disheartening because it not only negatively affects her, but it can negatively impact her students as well. We use this as a caveat to explain that we do not feel the CARE method or any method can be effective if the teacher does not possess this genuine care.

The C.A.R.E Model for Youth Culture Pedagogy

Culture
- Embrace Youth Culture

Affable
- Create an Affable Learning Environment

Relationships
- Build & Maintain Positive Relationships

Egalitarian
- Develop an Egalitarian Teaching Style

Now that you have been introduced to our C.A.R.E. Model, let us discuss how we will impart supporting evidence. We will lay the groundwork for our theoretical construct and, in each subsequent chapter, will give scenarios of how this theory can be applied to various educational situations that we, and undoubtedly, other educators have experienced on a daily basis. Through a theoretical framework of relational pedagogy and care, we will explore the tenets of YCP. In addition, we will demonstrate how YCP is rooted in the ideas of culturally relevant pedagogy, hip-hop based education and reality pedagogy. All of this leads to our belief that YCP should be placed as part of HHBE's second wave theory as advanced by Petchauer (2015).

MC Notes!

"We don't even gotta speak YCP and we do the same things YCP, we stay connected worldwide YCP, this is how we live life YCP, already changed the whole game YCP, we all know the same slang YCP, y'all better all get to know about YCP, It's Rawls and Robinson we building on YCP word Youth Culture Power."

When we say Youth Culture Power we are speaking directly about the brilliant and dynamic cultural power of young people around the world. We are talking about how young people are connected worldwide without even speaking to each other, seeing what each other are doing or even knowing one another and yet, they are in sync and on the same page. Young people around the world in more cases than not are listening to the same music, wearing the same fashion, watching the same content, know about the same things and have a lot of the same interests in general. These connections are not coincidence, luck or magic; well maybe a little magical, but it is important to understand how these connections relate to culture. Although many of these connections are directly related to hip-hop culture we understand that youth culture is even bigger than hip-hop culture because it describes the way young people live around the world whether they are directly in tune with hip-hop culture or not. Even when young people are not listening to Hip Hop/Rap music they are still usually participating in some capacity through fashion, media, film, sports and other things in their daily lives that directly connects to hip-hop culture.

It is important to realize that we are in a time where young people wake up to a global platform every day due to their engagement on the internet via gaming, social media, mobile apps, streaming music and more. These are just a few of the consistencies happening in youth culture that continues to cause both hip-hop and youth culture to grow exponentially around the world. Young people are cut from the cloth of being technologically savvy and next level, they were literally born into it. We feel it is very important for us adults to embrace this reality as well as encourage and nurture the tech savvy of the younger generation because we understand that the society and most of the jobs that standard education of today are preparing our students for won't exist by time they graduate. The world is run by technology and as we all move into the future it is becoming more pertinent to be in touch with technology, otherwise it will be very difficult to prosper in modern society. When I reflect on my own life and being here only 40 plus years on the planet I can't count how many things have changed around the world and in society in general since I was a youngster. However, one of the things I can say hasn't changed a great deal is school and that's scary to me because we are failing our youth. The main reason we feel so strongly about technology is because it is directly connected to youth culture in so many ways and we also recognize it as a strong entry point into the minds and hearts of the youth.

To give a direct example, in 2013 at Legal Studies High School in Brooklyn I was a part of an initiative helping prepare students for the Regents Exam, which is the Statewide Standardized Test in NY that every student must pass in at least 5 subjects to graduate. The students I worked with there for the span of 4 years for the most part entered the classroom after failing this exam more than a few times which in most cases caused a lack confidence and many broken spirits. A lot of these students were literally stuck in high school and at risk of aging out or dropping out because they could not pass this exam. The main class I taught there was Global History Prep and after learning how well versed the students were in social media and other things that were directly school related. I began to figure out the most productive and safest ways to bring some of these things into the classroom and use them with different activities. I would do things like have students fill out printed mock up Facebook pages or Instagram posts for famous historical characters and have student fill in the information based on their knowledge of the content. What would Nelson Mandela or Gandhi's (or any other historical figures) Facebook page look like? Who would be their friends? Where are they from? What would they post on Instagram? and the list goes on. I have even used Snapchat and Instagram stories to have students shoot video reenacting a historical event and then play it for the class and reflect on it. To be fair every single student will not participate right away, being patient and consistent is very important, respect the process. In my experience once students are able to either see themselves or something that connects to them in the work they are learning it changes their perspective of the content and now they are more willing to engage in the material. Once this happens my main objective is to have students create something art related around the content and now they can embody it and think critically about what they are learning. It is usually at these moments of learning that the students remember them forever.

It is important to address that we more than understand the significance of young people having fundamental knowledge of reading, writing, mathematics, science and other foundational academics. We also understand the pros and cons of young people and new technology; however, we are strong advocates for innovation and feel it is important to have a balance. Teachers today need to be more mindful of the power that lies within these cultural nuances that your students are carrying into the classroom every day. To this point, I had the amazing opportunity to present some of the concepts and ideas directly from the initial creations that would become this book you are reading right now at the #HipHopEd Conference in 2018 at Teachers College, Columbia University. During my workshop I asked a group of educators, scholars, parents, and students etc. to raise their hand if they ever heard the saying "On Fleek" and the entire room raised their hands. I then asked who knows where that saying comes from. And no one raised their hand, which was pretty shocking but also made lots of sense all at the same time. I further explained that the saying "On Fleek" was popularized from a 7 sec video posted on the social media platform called "VINE" by Kayla Newman a Chicago based teen who had just gotten her eyebrows done for the first time and boasted in the post "Eyebrows on Fleek" under the handle (@PeachesMonroee). Soon After the video went viral on the now defunct "Vine" platform and the saying "On Fleek" has landed in the bars of hip-hop mega stars Nicki Minaj and Cardi B to popular fashion designers graphic tees. It is important to see that not only did Kayla go viral with her saying "On Fleek" but she added on to culture and communication that crossed barriers around the world to impact many different types of people. These are some of the many reasons I am an advocate for young people around the world. I have witnessed their brilliance over and over and they still don't get the props and recognition they deserve for it.

During my initial trainings as a Teaching Artist in NYC a group of fellow TA's would meet up weekly under the guidance of educators and professors to talk about what the group coined "The Fleek of the Week. This was how we described what was the most popular content and happenings in Youth Culture and Popular Culture around the world. Some honorable mentions are of course the "On Fleek" video, Michael Jordan (Cry Face Emoji), Young Cardi B Memes, Kiki Dance Challenge and Fidget Spinners to name a few. We would all literally bring in what we felt was the "FLEEK of the Week" in the form of memes, hashtags, SMS abbreviations, videos, pics, emojis, social conflict, reality show drama, social media characters, youtubers and so much more and talk about the best ways to use it in the classroom safely and productive. This was the start of my first-hand experience of witnessing the brilliance and influence of young people around the world that still sits close to my heart to this very day. I began to see how things like SMS abbreviations were being used around the world by a diverse group of people although; young people worldwide popularized them. Just like what happens in Hip Hop Culture young people continue to create new ways of innovating how we communicate and connect to the world by using many tools and resources that have been here in ways that haven't been thought of or considered before them. Although we have heard so many adults criticize SMS abbreviations and other fast and efficient methods of young people communicating, we see this no different from the symbols and codes that were used in the highly advanced ancient civilizations like the Sumerians Cuneiform and the Egyptian Hieroglyphics. It is because of all of these things and so much more that we stand firm in our advocacy for young people as we scream out Youth Culture Power.

Audi 5000

How much power is really in youth culture? It really depends on you as the educator, administrator or parent. Are you in it for yourself or for your students? With this explanation of Youth Culture Pedagogy, we call this chapter (and the song it's named for) Youth Culture Power (YCP) because we believe in the power of youth culture. Youth culture is a powerful force and we believe that teachers can use it to help them gain an important perspective of students. Understanding cultural tropes that students embody, such as "on fleek" and the Michael Jordan crying face meme, provide educators a powerful peek into the world of young people. Using youth culture is like having a key to unlock some of the most powerful puzzles which are our youth. On several occasions, we have been asked "Well how do I find out about that world?" or "How can I dig into youth culture?" One of the most important ways to do this is to listen to young people. Let's discuss how that may look in the classroom.

References

Adjapong, E., & Emdin, C. (2015). Rethinking pedagogy in urban spaces: implementing hip-hop pedagogy in the urban science classroom. *Journal of Urban Learning Teaching and Research, 11*, 66–77.

Affability. (n.d.). In *Merriam-Webster's online dictionary* (11th ed.). Retrieved from http://www.m-w.com/dictionary/affability

Alim, H. S. (2007). Critical hip-hop language pedagogies: combat, consciousness, and the cultural politics of communication. *Journal of Language Identity and Education, 6*(2), 161–176.

Appiah, K. A. (2007). *Cosmopolitanism: Eethics in a world of strangers* (Issues of our time). New York, NY: W. W. Norton & Company.

Aspelin, J. (2011). Co-existence and co-operation: the two-dimensional conception of education. *Education, 1*(1), 6–11.

Baker, J. A., Grant, S., & Morlock, L. (2008). The teacher-student relationship as a developmental context for children with internalizing or externalizing behavior problems. *School Psychology Quarterly, 23*(1), 3–15.

Barile, J. P., Donohue, D. K., Anthony, E. R., Baker, A. M., Weaver, S. R., & Henrich, C. C. (2012). Teacher–student relationship climate and school outcomes: Implications for educational policy initiatives. *Journal of Youth and Adolescence, 41*(3), 256–267.

Beninghof, A. M. (2006). *Engage all students through differentiation.* Peterborough, NH: Crystal Springs Books.

Benn, G. (n.d.). What is H. E.L. P? Retrieved from http://www.edlyrics.com/whatishelp

Biesta, G. (2004). "Mind the Gap!": Communication and the educational relation. In C. Bingham & A. Sidorkin (Eds.) *No education without relation* (pp. 11–22). New York, NY: Peter Lang.

Blackman, S. (2005). Youth subcultural theory: A critical engagement with the concept, its origins and politics, from the Chicago school to postmodernism. *Journal of Youth Studies, 8*(1), 1–20.

Blackman, S. J. (2014). Subculture theory: an historical and contemporary assessment of the concept for understanding deviance. *Deviant Behavior, 35*(6), 496–512.

Buber, M. (1958). The I-thou theme, contemporary psychotherapy, and psychodrama. *Pastoral Psychology, 9*(5), 57–58.

Buber, M. (2003). *Between man and man.* New York, NY: Routledge.

Catt, S., Miller, D. & Schallenkamp, K. (2007). You are the key: Communicate for learning effectiveness. *Education, 127*(3), 369–377.

Chang, J. (2005). *Can't stop, won't stop: a history of the hip-hop generation.* New York, NY: St. Martin's Press.

Cherfas, L., Casciano, R., & Wiggins, M. A. (2018). It's bigger than hip-hop: Estimating the impact of a culturally responsive classroom intervention on student outcomes. *Urban Education, 1–34.*

Christenson, S., Reschly, A. L., & Wylie, C. (2012). *Handbook of research on student engagement.* New York, NY: Springer.

Clemmons, J. (2006). Rapport and motivation in the applied studio. *Journal of Singing, 63*(2), 205–210.

Compton-Lilly, C. (2007). What can video games teach us about teaching reading? *Reading Teacher, 60*, 718–727.

Culture. (n.d.). In *Merriam-Webster's online dictionary* (11th ed.). Retrieved from http://www.m-w.com/dictionary/culture

Delpit, L. D. (1995). *Other people's children: Cultural conflict in the classroom*. New York, NY: New Press.

Dimitriadis, G. (2001). *Performing identity/performing culture: Hip hop as text, pedagogy, and lived practice*. New York, NY: Peter Lang.

Dimitriadis, G. (2015). Framing hip hop: New methodologies for new times. *Urban Education, 50*(1), 31–50.

Docan-Morgan, T. (2009). A typology of relational turning point events in college teacher-student relationships. *Journal of Scholarship of Teaching and Learning, 9*(2), 82–97.

Doumen, S., Koomen, H. M. Y., Buyse, E., Wouters, S., & Verschueren, K. (2012). Teacher and observer views on student–teacher relationships: Convergence across kindergarten and relations with student engagement. *Journal of School Psychology, 50*, 61–76.

Duncan-Andrade, J. M. (2004). Your best friend or your worst enemy: youth popular culture, pedagogy, and curriculum in urban classrooms. *The Review of Education, Pedagogy and Cultural Studies, 26*, 313–337.

Duncan-Andrade, J. M., & Morrell, E. (2008). *The art of critical pedagogy: Possibilities for moving from theory to practice in urban schools*. New York, NY: Peter Lang.

Egalitarian. (n.d.). In *Merriam-Webster's online dictionary* (11th ed.). Retrieved from http://www.m-w.com/dictionary/egalitarian

[Elon University]. (2012, March 15). Christopher Emdin speaks to Elon teaching fellows [Video File]. Retrieved from https://www.youtube.com/watch?v=a9Ob2CRjh94

Emdin, C. (2009). Rethinking student participation: a model from hip-hop and urban science education. *Edge Phi Delta Kappa International, 5*(1), 1–18.

Emdin, C. (2011a). Citizenship and social justice in urban science education. *International Journal of Qualitative Studies in Education, 24*(3), 285–301.

Emdin, C. (2011b). Moving beyond the boat without a paddle: reality pedagogy, black youth, and urban science education. *The Journal of Negro Education, 80*(3), 284–295.

Emdin, C. (2016). *For white folks who teach in the hood: And the rest of y'all too*. Boston, MA: Beacon Press.

Emdin, C., Adjapong, E. (Eds.) (2018). *#Hiphoped: The compilation on hip-hop education—Vol. 1: Hip-hop as education, philosophy, and practice*. Leiden, The Netherlands: Brill/Sense Publishers.

Freire, P. (1970). *Pedagogy of the oppressed*. New York, NY: Continuum.

Frisby, B. N., & Martin, M. M. (2010). Instructor-student and student-instructor rapport in the classroom. *Communication Education, 59*(2), 146–164.

Frisby, B. N., & Myers, S. A., (2008). The relationships among perceived instructor rapport, student participation, and student learning outcomes. *Texas Speech Communication Journal, 33*(1), 27–34.

Fullan, M. (2003). *The moral imperative of school leadership*. Toronto: Corwin.

Gardner, H. (2011). *Frames of mind: The theory of multiple intelligences*. New York, NY: Basic Books.

Gardner, H. & Davis, K. (2013). *The app generation: how today's youth navigate identity, intimacy, and imagination in a digital world*. New Haven, CT: Yale University Press.

Gay, G. (2000). *Culturally responsive teaching: Theory, research, and practice*. New York, NY: Teachers College Press.

Gee, J. P. (2003). *What video games have to teach us about learning and literacy*. New York, NY: Palgrave Macmillan.

Gergen, K. J. (2009). *Relational being: Beyond self and community*. Oxford: Oxford University Press.

Giroux, H. A. (1989). *Schooling and the struggle for public life: Critical pedagogy in the modern age*. Minneapolis, MN: University of Minnesota Press.

Giroux, H. (2016). *America on the edge: Henry Giroux on politics, culture, and education*. New York, NY: Palgrave Macmillan.

Hall, T. D. (2007). *A pedagogy of freedom: Using hip hop in the classroom to engage African-American students* (Doctoral dissertation, University of Missouri-Columbia). Retrieved from https://mospace.umsystem.edu/xmlui/bitstream/handle/10355/4864/research. pdf?sequence=3

Hart, S. R., Stewart, K., & Jimerson, S. R. (2011). The student engagement in schools questionnaire (SESQ) and the teacher engagement report form-new (TERF-N): Examining the preliminary evidence. *Contemporary School Psychology: Formerly "The California School Psychologist," 15*(1), 67–79.

Hicks Harper, P. T. (2000, June/July). Understanding youth popular culture and the hip hop influence. *SIECUS Report, 28*(5), 19–23.

[High Tech Slam]. (2015, May 21). Hip-hop education: An interview with Dr. David Kirkland [Video File]. Retrieved from https://www.youtube.com/watch?v=FhM2q-5u9l8

Hill, M. L. (2009). *Beats, rhymes, and classroom life: Hip-hop pedagogy and the politics of identity*. New York, NY: Teachers College Press.

Hill, M. L., & Petchauer, E. (Eds.) (2015). Schooling hip-hop: Expanding hip-hop based education across the curriculum. New York, NY: Teachers College Press.

Hilliard, A. (2002). Language, culture and the assessment of African-American children. In L. D. Delpit & J. K. Dowdy (Eds.), *The skin that we speak: Thoughts on language and culture in the classroom* (pp. 87–105). New York, NY: New Press.

Hollie, S. (n.d.). *Infusing Culturally Responsive Instruction into Daily Teaching I | Sharroky Hollie—Academia.edu*. Retrieved from Professional Development Guidebook website: http://www.academia.edu/1041557/Infusing_Culturally_Responsive_Instruction_into_Daily_Teaching_I

Irby, D. (2015). Urban is floating face down in the mainstream: Using hip-hop based education research to resurrect "the urban" in urban education. *Urban Education, 50*(1), 7–30.

Irizarry, J. G. (2009). Representin': Drawing from hip-hop urban youth culture to inform teacher education. *Education and Urban Society, 41*(4), 489–515.

Janssen, J., Dechesne, M., & Van Knippenberg, A. (1999). The psychological importance of youth culture: a terror management approach. *Youth & Society, 31*, 152–167.

Jensen, S. (2016). Empathy and imagination in education for sustainability. *Canadian Journal of Environmental Education, 21*, 89–105.

Jones, R. D. (2008). Strengthening student engagement. *International Center for Leadership in Education, 1*.

Kim, Y., & Wei, Q. (2011). The impact of learner attributes and learner choice in an agent-based environment. *Computers & Education, 56*(2), 505–514.

Ladson-Billings, G. (1994). *The dreamkeepers: Successful teachers of African American children*. San Francisco, CA: Jossey-Bass Publishers.

Ladson-Billings, G. (1995a). But that's just good teaching! The case for culturally relevant pedagogy. *Theory into Practice, 34*(3), 159–165.

Ladson-Billings, G. (1995b). Toward a theory of culturally relevant pedagogy. *American Educational Research Journal, 32*(3), 465–491.

Ladson-Billings, G. (2014). Culturally relevant pedagogy 2.0 a.k.a. the remix. *Harvard Educational Review, 84*(1), 74–84.

Lindsey, T. (2015). Let me blow your mind: Hip hop feminist futures in theory and praxis. *Urban Education, 50*(1), 52–77.

Love, B. (2015). What is hip-hop-based education doing in nice fields such as early childhood and elementary education? *Urban Education, 50*(1), 106–131.

Mahiri, J. (2001). Pop culture pedagogy and the end(s) of school. *Journal of Adolescent & Adult Literacy, 44*(4), 382–85.

Mahiri, J. (2006). Digital DJ-ing: Rhythms of learning in an urban school. *Language Arts, 84*(1), 55–62.

Mania, B., & Janiak, J. (Producers) (2018, January 28). *Sunday TODAY with Willie Geist* [Television broadcast]. New York, NY: NBC/Universal.

Margonis, F. (1999a). The demise of authenticity. In S. Tozer (Ed.), *Philosophy of education: 1998* (pp. 248–257). Urbana, IL: Philosophy of Education Society.

Margonis, F. (1999b). Relational pedagogy without foundations: Reconstructing the work of Paulo Freire. *Philosophy of Education Archive*, 99–107.

McLaren, P. (1989). *Life in schools: An introduction to critical pedagogy in the foundations of education*. New York, NY: Longman.

McIntyre, H. (2017, July 17). Report: Hip-hop/R&B is the dominant genre in the U.S. for the first time. Retrieved from https://www.forbes.com/sites/hughmcintyre/2017/07/17/hip-hoprb-has-now-become-the-dominant-genre-in-the-u-s-for-the-first-time/#672144055383

Milner, H. R. (2011). Culturally relevant pedagogy in a diverse urban classroom. *Urban Review, 43*, 66–89.

Mojab, S. & Taber, N. (2015). Memoir pedagogy: Gender narratives of violence and survival. *The Canadian Journal for the Study of Adult Education, 27*(2), 31–45.

Morrell, E. (2002). Toward a critical pedagogy of popular culture: Literacy development among urban youth. *Journal of Adolescent & Adult Literacy, 46*(1), 72–77.

Morrell, E., & Duncan-Andrade, J. M. (2002). Promoting academic literacy with urban youth through engaging hip-hop culture. *The English Journal, 91*(6), 88–92.

Noddings, N. (2002). *Educating moral people: A caring alternative to character education*. New York, NY: Teachers College Press.

Noddings, N. (2005). *The challenge to care in schools: An alternative approach to education* (2nd ed.). New York, NY: Teachers College Press.

Paris, D. (2012). Culturally sustaining pedagogy: A needed change in stance, terminology, and practice. *Educational Researcher, 41*(3), 93–97.

Petchauer, E. (2009). Framing and reviewing hip-hop educational research. *Review of Educational Research, 79*(2), 946–978.

Petchauer, E. (2010). Sampling practices and social spaces: Exploring a hip hop approach to higher education. *Journal of College Student Development, 51*(4), 359–372.

Petchauer, E. (2011). I feel what he was doin': Responding to justice-oriented teaching through hip-hop aesthetics. *Urban Education, 46*(6), 1411–1432.

Petchauer, E. (2012). *Hip-hop culture in college students' lives: Elements, embodiment, and higher edutainment.* New York, NY: Routledge.

Petchauer, E. (2015). Starting with style: Toward a second wave of hip-hop education research and practice. *Urban Education, 50*(1), 78–105.

Pianta, R. C. (1999). *Enhancing relationships between children and teachers.* Washington, DC: American Psychological Association.

Porfilio, B. J., & Carr, P. R. (2010). *Youth culture, education and resistance subverting the commercial ordering of life.* Rotterdam: Sense Publishers.

Rawls, J. D. (2017). *We relate because we care: A case study on teacher student relations and care in a hip-hop based education classroom.* (Dissertation). Retrieved from ProQuest Dissertations and Theses database.

Richmond, V. (1990). Communication in the classroom: power and motivation. *Communication Education, 39*, 181–195.

Rodríguez, L. F. (2009). Dialoguing, cultural capital, and student engagement: Toward a hip hop pedagogy in the high school and university classroom. *Equity & Excellence in Education, 42*(1), 20–35.

Rutherford, N. (2017). Fidget spinners: the new craze in school playgrounds. *BBC.* Retrieved from http://www.bbc.com/news/uk-scotland-39778578

Sandlin, J. A., & Milam, J. L. (2008). Mixing pop (culture) and politics: Cultural resistance, culture jamming, and anti-consumption activism as critical public pedagogy. *Curriculum Inquiry, 38*(3), 323–350.

Shildrick, T. (2006). Youth culture, subculture and the importance of neighbourhood. *Young, 14*(1), 61–74.

Sidorkin, A. M. (2000). *Toward a Pedagogy of Relation.* Retrieved from http://digitalcommons.ric.edu/facultypublications/17

Sidorkin, A. M. (2002). *Learning relations: Impure education, deschooled schools, and dialogue with evil.* New York, NY: Peter Lang.

Stuhlman, M., & Pianta, R. (2002). Teachers' narratives about their relationships with children: associations with behavior in classrooms. *School Psychology Review, 31*(2) 148–163.

Stovall, D. (2006). We can relate: Hip-hop culture, critical pedagogy, and the secondary classroom. *Urban Education, 41*(6), 585–602.

Sull, E. C. (2009). Student engagement, motivation, and rapport. *Distance Learning, 6*(3), 90–94.

Tuck, E., & Yang, K. W. (2014). *Youth resistance research and theories of change.* New York, NY: Routledge, Taylor & Francis Group.

[UMH Hurley Convergence Center]. (2017, April 6). Dr. Gloria Ladson-Billings, "Hip hop, hip hope: Reinventing culturally relevant pedagogy" [Video File]. Retrieved from https://www.youtube.com/watch?v=oj4z6AQj9zA

Veel, L., & Bredhauer, M. (2009). 'Living local, thinking global': Creating and sustaining pedagogies. *International Journal of Learning, 16*(9), 597–610.

Wallaert, K. A., & Wessel, R. D. (2011). Student perceptions of the hip hop culture's influence on the undergraduate experience. *Journal of College Student Development, 52*(2), 162–179.

White, J. (2009). Sustainable pedagogy: a research narrative about teachers, creativity and performativity. *TCI (Transnational Curriculum Inquiry), 5*(1), 58–70.

Willis, P. (2002). *Common culture: Symbolic work at play in the everyday cultures of the young.* Milton Keynes: Open University Press.

Wilson, J. H., Ryan, R. G., & Pugh, J. L. (2010). Professor-student rapport scale predicts student outcomes. *Teaching of Psychology, 37*, 246–251.

Yosso, T. J. (2005). Whose culture has capital? A critical race theory discussion of community cultural wealth. *Race Ethnicity and Education, 8*(1), 69–91.

Young, E. (2010). Challenges to conceptualizing and actualizing culturally relevant pedagogy: How viable is the theory in classroom practice? *Journal of Teacher Education, 61*(3), 248–260.

· 2 ·

CLASSROOM CHATTER

"See this Chatter is their voice, their expressions, that same Chatter is what taught me these lessons, I learn things like who barely slept last night because their parents are having issues and had a REAL BIG FIGHT! …"

Say What?

As an educator, do you allow your students to speak or socialize in your classroom? One issue that teacher's struggle with is student chatter within the classroom. Some teachers allow this (even if at certain times within the class period), while others never allow this chatter to take place. Some teachers will tell you that allowing this chatter will disrupt your class and can even lead to the class becoming unruly. As a matter of principle, they will tell you that allowing students to have conversations in the classroom shows signs of bad classroom management. The topic of classroom management is generally mentioned alongside the principles of behaviorist frameworks. However, my research primarily focuses on teacher-student relationships through pedagogy of relation (Bingham & Sidorkin, 2004; Sidorkin, 2002). Teacher's, using an ethic of care (Noddings, 2002), develop lasting, meaningful relationships with students. Once these relationships are established and NURTURED, classroom management becomes an almost autonomous task. Thus, the bulk of my research connects relationships as a method of classroom management. The next several chapters will discuss relationships and care more in depth.

In this chapter, we will associate the idea of using pedagogy of relation to help foster and promote the idea of student voice within the classroom setting. While we still assert that there are times during class that students must be listening and paying attention to instructions, we will primarily focus on those seminal times at the end (or the beginning, or middle) of class in which we give our students time to talk. We will explore an alternative viewpoint of student conversation during class. We acquiesce to acceptance rather than scoffing at this chatter in the classroom, it can be incorporated as a means of building relationships and encouraging student voice. When properly designated and sanctioned, classroom chatter can garner teachers a wealth of information from which relationships can be solidified. We will also discuss the notion that this classroom chatter is a normal component of social interaction which precludes a sense of belonging. Lastly, we will discuss why a classroom setting should be enjoyable for students. Why is there no emphasis on making the classroom enjoyable? We will discuss how these normal human characteristics can be advantageous in a classroom setting.

We must preface this chapter with a clarifying caveat. By no means are we advocating that there should be no accountability or consequences in classrooms or in schools. However, we reject behaviorist policies which solely rely on a stimulus-response formula to education (Smyth, 2006). We feel that social interaction promotes a sense of belonging which effects student perceptions of their classroom and may even have an effect on academic outcomes. For these reasons, we feel reform is necessary.

What's the Deal?

Currently, the American education system is rooted in a data-driven and behavioristic methodology which is prescribed by punitive and systemic polices (Smyth, 2006). We support a shift in the current behavioristic approach to education. Our reasoning is based on my prior qualitative research and our own experiences of working with students. In accordance with Klem and Connell (2004), we feel that three main characteristics of a classroom are necessary in order for students to be successful:

1. Students need to feel cared for and have strong relationships with teachers in their classroom.
2. Students should feel like they are able to make decisions that involve them and their class; student voice.
3. Finally, students need structure and routine within the classroom. (p. 262)

In our classrooms, we set routines and have a set structure in place for students (more on this later). We also require high expectations in the classroom and back that up with meaningful relationships. The emphasis on the relationships is what gives us the leverage in the classroom to require those high expectations. When our students enter the classroom, we greet them. We ask them how their day is going so far, we make normal conversation with them. As students walk into the classroom and they are greeted, the structures that are in place, such as a bell ringer or a specific duty, allow them to feel a part of the classroom community. This works because students have a sense of belonging and a feeling of community. This sense of belonging is all part of relationship building that we feel enables our students to feel like they are a part of a community. It is for this reason that we prescribe to an approach of pedagogy of relation. It is our belief that this approach best lends itself to creating a communal setting within our classrooms.

As previously stated, we believe that care is one of the most important aspects to teaching. Defining care is no easy task, but we rely on Noddings (2002) explanation of caring in schools. Noddings (1984) explains that care can be broken down into two concepts; natural caring (a moral attitude that does not require an ethical stance to motivate it) and ethical caring (which is "rooted in receptivity, relatedness, and responsiveness") (p. 2). She further explains that in order for one to have care, three items must occur: First, receptive attention, meaning that the carer listens to what the cared for wants. In other words, there is a cyclical relationship in which the person caring hears the voice of the person being cared for. Second, the person being cared for must be receptive to and acknowledge the caring action. Finally, Noddings (2002) suggests that both parties must gain from the encounter. Noddings' (2002, 2005) concept of "caring for" (encounters in which one person cares directly for another individual) and "caring about" (when one cares for others simply because they are human beings) (Noddings, 2002) informs how a teacher cares for her students. Teachers using an ethic of care in order to create a sense of connectedness "are the theoretical constructs that take human relationships to the primary building blocks of reality" (Sidorkin, 2000, p. 1). This posture of care embraces teacher characteristics that focus more on the individual student and supports that the teacher's own moral responsibility eventually leads to a sense of social justice (Noddings, 2005). We use a simple example of greeting students when they enter your classroom as a first step to showing care. A greeting is also a great way to break the ice and start the conversational process toward pedagogy of relation.

The relevance of pedagogy of relation is paramount as it leads to intrinsic learning through students' mutual sharing of stories or dialogue within the classroom. Sidorkin (2002) describes these stories as real experiences shared between the teacher and students in the classroom in a manner in which students feel free to participate with stories about their lives and experiences. His idea that students need something else besides knowledge from school can be considered a radical notion. However, we feel that this is the right path to shifting the behavioristic approach in schools to one focused on relationships. With a pedagogy of relation, the level of coercion in schools is decreased because the student voice is heard, and teachers use a polyphonic form of authority. In his classroom, students gain more than just intellect from school because they are an essential piece to the learning process. While there are several ways to include students as part of this process, using aspects of youth culture (including Hip-Hop) in the classroom is a method that can allow the classroom to become a forum for the student voice. YCP is once such method because it proposes using youth culture as an equal asset within the classroom. Thus, YCP aligns with Sidorkin's (2002) classroom as a novel approach to relational pedagogy.

Shevalier and McKenzie (2012) extend these ideas suggesting that teaching should encompass care ethics and inquiry to form solid relationships. This aligns seamlessly with both Sidorkin's (2002) and Noddings' (2002) theories. They expand on this, adding that the goal of CRP "is to respond to students in ways that build positive relationships" (Shevalier & McKenzie, 2012, p. 6). Noddings (2002) conception of "caring for" supports this formation of solid relationships in the classroom. The result of teachers caring for students can translate into students who eventually "care about" others in their community, which leads to a sense of social justice.

Smyth (2006) adds on to this idea of relationships stating "when we fail to place relationships at the center of schooling … then we fail in one of our most fundamental responsibilities as citizens in a democracy" (p. 4). Smyth (2006) goes on to add that schools are inherently a "relationally rich" environment in which social interactions are at the heart of what it means to be in school (p. 5). Part of implementing an idea of social justice within students is encouraging them that "they can do it" and that they are power-ful people (Smyth, 2006, p. 4). Teachers who embolden students with these positive words and allow them to have a voice are adding on to this notion of formulating students into global citizens. This aligns with our egalitarian concept from the C.A.R.E. Method. Teachers who are proponents of student voice naturally seek to create equality in their classroom.

Once again, we agree that student's need structure and routine in the classroom. From our point of view, all human beings operate better when a routine is in place to help navigate through life's twists and turns. Imple-menting structure and routine as part of classroom management is not new. Researchers have long theorized that structure and routine are imperative to controlling classroom behavior (Klem & Connell, 2004; Leinhardt, Weid-man & Hammond, 1987; Simonsen, Fairbanks, Briesch, Myers & Sugai, 2008). Most of the methods given to deal with classroom management issues are based on behavior methodologies. This is evidenced as Simonsen et al. (2008) insist that classroom management can also be used to "promote more appropriate academic and social behavior" (p. 357). However, it seems as if implanting these policies as a part of a behaviorist framework can sometimes be oppressive and intimidating. When these policies are implemented using a YCP approach they can still align with ideas of Sidorkin (2002) and Noddings (2002). Using YCP to implement structure and routine is less insensitive and usually delineates longer lasting results.

What's the Science?

So what's the science? The science is applying a pedagogy of youth culture. YCP allows student voice to be heard. This research has high implications for our purposes of implementing YCP into one's classroom. Allowing students some time to socially interact in one's class on a regular basis aligns with an ethic of care, pedagogy of relation and embracing chattering students (Nod-dings, 2002; Sandstrom & Dunn, 2014; Sidorkin, 2002). Youth culture theory aligns with this notion that students who are allowed to socially interact in the classroom feel a sense of belonging, seem to enjoy the class more and ulti-mately have better grades as a result.

With these three main characteristics in mind, we believe a discussion is warranted on how classroom chatter could possibly be viewed as a positive within a classroom setting. While admittedly there has not been much research on the topic of chattering students, we believe that this could be an untapped wealth of relational strategy. Sandstrom and Dunn (2014) speak about some of these redeeming qualities in their study about chattering students. Their study explores the benefits of classroom chatter in the forms of student voice, social interaction and promoting feelings of belonging. Inevitably, students have better perceptions about a class when they are allowed to socially interact within that classroom. We agree with this premise. In our past experiences, students and any person in general, tend to have a more favorable view of any activity in which they are able to be social with others. Sandstrom and Dunn (2014) further argue that "student-to-student interactions, even when off-topic, serve to build a sense of belonging which … improves students' perceptions of the class … and may even improve student learning" (p. 1). In their study, Sandstrom and Dunn (2014) found that when students were able to interact socially, they had a more favorable opinion of the class in general. Students in the study also seemed to feel that they learned more. Although, this last scenario was not tested, it permeates well with the idea that student perception of the class is directly related to learning in the classroom.

Faircloth (2009) links aspects of social interaction with belonging and identity among youth. In fact, this study found a strong connection between how students see themselves, their culture and issues that they found important to belonging. Students within the classroom glean important benefits from conversation with others and at times, this conversation could generate positive outcomes. Research shows that even interactions with those who we consider acquaintances still have an effect on our sense of belonging (Clay, 2003; Duncan, 2011; Sandstrom & Dunn, 2014).

In addition to belonging, students reported a greater sense of enjoyment when they were allowed time to converse in the classroom (Sandstrom & Dunn, 2014). Frenzel, Goetz, Ludtke, Pekrum and Sutton (2009) found that teacher enjoyment of a class and student enjoyment of the same class are positively linked. In addition, teacher enthusiasm and tolerance adjudicate student enjoyment in the classroom. With this in mind, YCP is relevant because adding aspects of youth culture to one's pedagogical approach promotes an enjoyable time for the student. Based on our experiences, students appreciate having things they value at the center of one's teaching method. With some social interaction, belonging and enjoyment present in the classroom, the effect on grades is noticeable (Sandstrom & Dunn, 2014).

All of the above ideas align with the concept of building relationships with students. Teachers who seek to build relationships can gain helpful information about their students just by listening to what they are talking about in the classroom. We call this 'listening with an open ear.' In our song "Classroom Chatter," we verbalize that teachers should mostly just listen. What we mean by this is, pay attention to what is going on in your classroom. Observe what your students are doing, who they speak to and the topics about which they speak. Allow students to speak about what is on their mind. This can give you subtle and sometimes very noticeable opportunities to make a difference in your classroom.

As previously mentioned, our goal here is to shift the current paradigm of education as a function of behaviors to one of relationships. As a teacher or even administrator in buildings with young adolescents, it may be a good idea to reconsider the role that classroom chatter plays within your pedagogical sphere. Students who enjoy your classroom are much easier to manage and there is a possible link to better grades. The sense of belonging and greater sense of enjoyment ultimately affect student grades.

MC Notes!

One of the things I learned early in my teaching practice is to always value the voices and culture of students in the classroom. I never walk into an urban school classroom and expect it to be completely quiet, and if it ever were completely quiet, class I would assume there is something wrong. I relate to my students mainly because I see myself in them and I remember being a student in New York City public schools growing up. I too saw a lot of harsh reality outside of the school just like I know they do. I understand that they are a part of the Hip-Hop Generation and how they express themselves is different, individualistic, innovative and constantly evolving. I also understand when these students get to school and want to talk about things happening in their lives that are great or even vent about not so great things that are happening as well.

I always expect some chatter before and at the end of class and I never spend a bunch of time quieting down my students. In my opinion, it kills the vibe and doesn't make the space feel welcoming. I let the students chat in the beginning of class and by doing so it allows the students to settle in and allows me to better understand the mood of the class. While this is happening, I always learn about so many different things going on in my student's lives. Before classroom chatter became something I purposely paid attention to, I realize now that it always served as a gauge for knowing when to take the empathetic approach with students. In school, I've witnessed what it is like when a student was arrested, hurt or even murdered. Students are never given the space and time to unpack these harsh realities that they witness and deal with every day. It is safe to say this classroom chatter is my blueprint or guideline to understanding my students more and I directly use much of this information in class as a solid entry point to raise student engagement and build community and relationships.

Classroom Chatter is my inside look directly into youth culture. I didn't have to guess about what was "in" when it came to young people I got it directly from them. Many times I took the fly on the wall approach by simply greeting my students as they entered the classroom, then allowing them to get settled and chatter for the first 3–5 minutes of class, and during this time I was purposely listening to my students to learn from them. The best way for me to transition back to getting class started after this chatter time was to have something youth culture based and was something they wouldn't see in most traditional classroom settings. A great example would be showing the class a meme, image, video or other youth culture based item relating to the lesson for the day. This has always been a solid entry point as it gets some critical thinking and conversations going on in class before the lesson even starts. Other times I would probe the students for what I wanted to know by turning it into an activity. One example of this is the activity **"FACTS OR NAH?"** which I will discuss later in this chapter.

After several weeks of purposely listening to the chatter, I began to use different lessons that included video, images, music, memes, #hash tags, stand up activities and other youth culture centered materials that I had learned about from the chatter. I am able to connect with the students in so many dynamic ways mainly due to the students observing that I make a genuine effort to engage them with things they are already familiar with. Students can easily see my willingness to be open minded in my approach to reach them more effectively. Later this developed into further understanding the importance of knowing the students I was teaching in class, which is very similar to performing live. The best way to engage an audience at a live show is to know your crowd. I noticed some students were more visual learners and anytime I brought in images or video they shined in that class. Other students were more kinesthetic learners with great body intelligence and they shined whenever I brought in an activity that involved getting up out of their seats and moving around. Still, there were also students who were very shy and reserved but they read and write extremely well and have excellent auditory skills. As long as they can hear it they will understand it.

I think it is important to acknowledge that I never announce or make the students directly aware about the "chatter time." It is just something that happened early on in my teaching experience which I began to do on purpose once I saw the benefits. In one of my earliest teaching experiences, my co-teacher sent me a text letting me know she was running 5–10 minutes late coming back from lunch. Since this was about ten minutes before class, it meant that I would need to start the class. As students entered the classroom I overheard them talking about the NBA Finals and Lebron James vs. Stephon Curry, another side of the classroom students were talking about their favorite YouTubers like D and B Nation, Ar'mon and Trey, Chris and Queen and more. Some other students were talking about gaming and the types of video games they were playing at the time like Fort Night, NBA 2K and Call of Duty etc. I was able to start with an activity that made mention of some of these topics I had heard from them earlier. The point of this story is that by simply listening to the chatter I learned so much about my classroom and the students in it. In return I was able to find out what materials would interest my students and what are the things young people are excited about or concerned about at the moment. Subsequently, I am also able to cater my delivery based on the mood and vibe of the classroom and this is an important part of my teaching practice, I am always prepared to switch up my delivery based on the mood if need be.

In addition to this being a great way to better connect with my students; I also realized that we are in a time where young people around the world witness the most traumatic situations via the news media, social media and other outlets. In the past several years many young people in America have learned about (and lived through) countless morbid violent incidents where the victims of these injustices are people of color. Several examples are the murders of Trayvon Martin, Mike Brown, Tamir Rice, Eric Garner, Korryn Gaines, Freddie Gray and so many more as well as the mysterious deaths of Sandra Bland and Kenneka Jenkins. More recently students witnessed video online of the murders of Philando Castile, Lesandro "Junior" Guzman-Feliz, XXXtentacion and the list unfortunately goes on and on. I noticed that although young people are immersed in all of this harsh and intense reality, they have absolutely nowhere to express how they feel about it all. Many of our students walk around with these feelings held inside and we wonder why some of our youth are so angry and intense at times. I truly feel that one of the many reasons for this behavior and other behavior issues is students not having an outlet to express their feelings. With this in mind, I always make it a point to create a space where students felt safe enough to express themselves and unpack these types of feelings and more.

I truly feel that without ever taking time to listen to the chatter I would not have been able to connect with my students in this same way. Classroom chatter is the direct voice of your students expressing the many things impacting their lives every day both positive and negative. Listening to the chatter in the classroom is a great way to empower yourself with the information needed to engage and connect with your students in a more powerful way.

Ideas to Use Chatter in Your Classroom

One way I engage and connect with my students is by lesson planning around things I hear students speaking about in the classroom, the hallways, at lunch, during recess. Some examples of lesson plans that came directly from chatter are as follows: Facts or Nah?, Bag of Questions, Immigration, The Black Panther Film (Wakanda), Police Shootings of Innocent people of Color, NBA FINALS, Super Bowl, YouTubers, the latest dances, Fidget spinners and much more. I will share a few of these lesson planning ideas below. The bottom line is the CHATTER MATTERS. Do yourself a huge favor. Listen and learn because it works wonders and can be a great resource to help in building solid and genuine relationships with your students.

Facts or Nah?

"Facts or Nah?" is a true or false based activity in which students move to a designated side of the classroom based on their responses to statements like "Snap chat is my favorite social media platform!" or "I feel safe and ready to learn in school," or something like "When I listen to music I focus mainly on the Lyrics." There are a variety of things I would ask them to learn what was on their minds; I always include school subjects in the various activities to see how students comprehend the material being taught.

Bag of Questions

Another example is an activity I call **"Bag of Questions?"** which is something I do when I am meeting students for the first time. In this activity, I walk around the classroom with folded strips of paper with questions on them inside a bag. Students are prompted to pick a question out the bag and then we go around the room allowing students to share their answers. These questions cover a wide range of items like "Where is your family from?" or "If I gave you a FREE plane ticket to anywhere in the world, where would you go?" or even "If you were in charge of school for a week, what changes would you make?" All of these different ice breaker/relationship building activities are aimed toward one common goal of making the classroom a safe space where the students feel comfortable sharing and learning.

Miscellaneous Ideas to Use Classroom Chatter

Some other methods that developed from classroom chatter include allowing students to chat for the final 5–10 minutes of class as long as all of the work for the day is completed. This portion of class sometimes is spent reflecting on the lesson being taught or something that is happening in the world that is important to the students. Another sure shot way for me to get the class started after the students settle in is using the most popular instrumentals of music the students are listening to. My technique is to turn it up to let the class get into it and then slowly turn it down and begin class now that I have everyone's attention. Also, creating a call and response chant works well for me. A direct example of this would be something like "When I say Mic Check, you say 1,2,1,2" and the entire class responded with "1,2,1,2" in unison.

However, one important aspect to remember is to be flexible. One time, I tried the "Mic Check" with a group of my 7th graders with lackluster results. They would not be into it. They told me that it felt too "old school." So I decided to ask the students what call and response would they like to do. My class decided they wanted to use a chant they heard on a Red Robin restaurant commercial. So whenever I said "Red Robin" the entire class responded "YUMMM!" and they were ready to go once I had their attention. The real funny thing about this is the fact that when I asked the class to raise their hand and tell me how many of them had visited a Red Robin restaurant, NO hands were raised. None of my class had even eaten at Red Robin, but they ALL knew the commercial and they all responded to it. The call and response method is something that when activated properly allows the entire class to join in and feel connected as one and it's a fun way to continue to build community in the classroom.

Audi 5000

Do you pay attention to your classroom chatter? Will that chatter help you in your classroom? It really depends on you. Are you in it for yourself or for your students? Think about the many times you have caught slight whisper of your student's conversation. Did you hear their ideas, challenges, fears, or maybe even trouble brewing? Just giving them a chance to speak freely, whether in a classroom or one-on-one setting can provide powerful insight into their views on the world around them. Giving students a chance to express their feelings in the classroom with an activity like "Facts or Nah" or "Bag of questions" is a wonderful catalyst for discussion. Allowing students a few minutes at the end of class a few times a week is also another good way to discover valuable information that could have an effect on the climate of your classroom. Having a heads up on these views is most important for a teacher because it allows you to plan and advocate for students as needed.

We get teachers that often ask us, "Well, I am concerned about letting them talk freely, because they eventually get too rowdy" or "How can I give them time to talk and still manage my classroom. In the next chapter, we will discuss how to implement these ideas using the principle foundation of YCP. It is not an easy task and may call for a need to change mindsets. But it is doable. Read on.

Interlude 1: Words from Dr. Ladson-Billings

While we were researching for this book, we found much solace in the words from Dr. Ladson-Billings. Her book *The Dreamkeepers* was revolutionary because it documented how *African-American teachers* achieved some measurable success teaching *African-American students*. Dr. Ladson-Billings study suggested that culture in the classroom mattered. The teachers in these classrooms believed in their students and truly thought that their students could be successful. The teachers were more like coaches or guides. They also recognized the importance of community within the classroom and consistently sought input from parents, community members and students. Moreover, these teachers took a familial approach to teaching and had an in-depth knowledge of their students. Ladson-Billings summed her ideas by saying that teachers need to understand the central role of culture in education. These are all important distinctions for our theoretical approach.

These ideas all coincide with our ideas on education. But we thought we should take it one step further. Of course similar to Ladson-Billings, Gay,

Delpit and others, we believe that culture should be an essential tool in an educator's arsenal. However, our main premise is that as teachers, we must strive to understand youth culture and weave this into our pedagogical practices. The idea behind this logic is quite simple. If we as educators understand the habits and customs of our students, we are better equipped to meet them where they are in their understanding of the world around them. Once we can do this, we can impart the knowledge that we want to share in a method that they can understand.

One of the easiest ways for us to do this is through hip-hop. Hip-hop is very prevalent in youth culture today. Ladson-Billings seems to agree. In a recent speech, she explains that after twenty-five years her ideas on CRP are evolving. She explains that youth culture, specifically, hip-hop can play a significant role in connecting with new century students, who we call Generation Z students (see chapter 4). These sentiments echo our need for teachers to delve into youth culture and incorporate it into classrooms. If we fail to see the importance of youth culture, as Dr. Ladson-Billings says, we risk losing a generation of students. We feel that is unacceptable.

References

Bingham, C. W., & Sidorkin, A. M. (2004). Let's treat authority relationally. In Charles Bingham & Alexander M. Sidorkin (Eds.), *No education without relation* (pp. 23–38). New York, NY: Peter Lang.

Clay, A. (2003). Keepin' it real Black youth, hip-hop culture, and black identity. *American Behavioral Scientist, 46*(10), 1346–1358.

Duncan, A. C. (2011). *Doing my thing, my way, for my purpose: Hip hop and African American student engagement*. Retrieved from Kweli Educational Enterprises website: http://education.uci.edu/docs/Duncan_2011AERA_abstract.pdf

Faircloth, B. S. (2009). Making the most of adolescence. *Journal of Adolescent Research, 24*(3), 321–348.

Frenzel, A. C., Goetz, T., Lüdtke, O., Pekrun, R., & Sutton, R. E. (2009). Emotional transmission in the classroom: Exploring the relationship between teacher and student enjoyment. *Journal of Educational Psychology, 101*(3), 705–716.

Klem, A. M., & Connell, J. P. (2004). Relationships matter: Linking teacher support to student engagement and achievement. *Journal of School Health, 74*(7), 262–273.

Leinhardt, G., Weidman, C., & Hammond, K. M. (1987). Introduction and integration of classroom routines by expert teachers. *Curriculum Inquiry, 17*(2), 135.

Noddings, N. (1984). *Caring: A feminine approach to ethics and moral education*. Berkeley, CA: University of California Press.

Noddings, N. (2002). *Educating moral people: A caring alternative to character education.* New York, NY: Teachers College Press.

Noddings, N. (2005). *The challenge to care in schools: An alternative approach to education* (2nd ed.). New York, NY: Teachers College Press.

Sandstrom, G. M., & Dunn, E. W. (2014). Social interactions and well-being. *Personality and Social Psychology Bulletin, 40*(7), 910–922.

Shevalier, R., & McKenzie, B. A. (2012). Culturally responsive teaching as an ethics-and care-based approach to urban education. *Urban Education, 20*(10), 1–20.

Sidorkin, A. M. (2000). *Toward a Pedagogy of Relation.* Retrieved from http://digitalcommons.ric.edu/facultypublications/17

Sidorkin, A. M. (2002). *Learning relations: Impure education, deschooled schools, and dialogue with evil.* New York, NY: Peter Lang.

Simonsen, B., Fairbanks, S., Briesch, A., Myers, D., & Sugai, G. (2008). Evidence-based practices in classroom management: Considerations for research to practice. *Education and Treatment of Children, 31*(1), 351–380.

Smyth, J. (2006). 'When students have power': student engagement, student voice, and the possibilities for school reform around 'dropping out' of school. *International Journal of Leadership in Education, 9*(4), 285–298.

· 3 ·

DON'T SMILE TILL NOVEMBER

"Imagine greeting all your students with genuine love vibes, and teaching them how to express what's hidden inside, their deepest thoughts and emotions so they can clarify and share their perspective with peers and watch it magnify ..."

Say What?

Classroom management is probably one of the most important pieces to K–12 classroom education. It seems that everyone has an opinion on how it should work, what philosophies should be used and when the best times are to implement a behavior plan in the classroom. According to Canter (1989) since the 1970's, teachers have been taught strategies such as "Don't smile until Christmas" or "if your curriculum is good enough, you won't have to worry about behavior (p. 58). Morris (n.d.) re-visits the idea in his blog liking it to traditional classroom management tactics. While some will say these are an old adage, others will tell you that seasoned teachers are encouraging pre-service teachers to follow some of these rigid procedures to maintain order in their classrooms. An important assumption of such a procedure is that the most important aspect of teaching is maintaining control of the classroom (Redman, 2005). Speaking from personal experience, pre-service teachers are not trained in many classroom management strategies.

While they are generally given strategies to manage classroom behavior during pre-service course work, it is very difficult for them to conceptualize how this will actually look until their first field experience. At which time, they are generally indoctrinated by their lead teacher. According to Martin, Yin and Mayall (2006), pre service teachers have inexperienced notions on classroom management which result in the use of survival skills during times of crisis. Often times, they are shown how to manage a class by a teacher who emphasizes behavior management. In contrast, we believe that students must feel cared for and teachers must strive to forge meaningful relationships with students. Care and relationships can be the most powerful tool in a teacher's arsenal. While there may always be extraneous issues or unforeseen circumstances, when care and relationships are demonstrated in the classroom, behavior management and increased student outcomes and engagement occur more fluidly. We also believe that teachers exhibiting care and building relationships delineates development of the whole child and is not only an important tenet of teaching, but should be a moral obligation. We acquiesce that pre-service teachers should be presented with these alternative methods for classroom management rooted in relational pedagogy and care ethics.

With respect to relationships and care, we also believe that as educators, we have a moral obligation to care for the whole child. According to Miller (1997), this holistic view completely defies our societal views of individualistic advances. In his view, teachers inherently choose a moral path to commit to developing the whole-child. This also intersects with a cosmopolitan approach to interpersonal relationships. Appiah (2007) describes cosmopolitanism as our moral obligation to have mutual respect for one another despite differing beliefs and cultures. Therefore, a pedagogy of relation ultimately leads to the belief that education is a benefit for the whole world, not just the individual and it should be a spiritual experience (Appiah, 2007; Miller, 1997; Palmer 2003). Fullan (2003) further supports this belief, declaring that teacher passion, purpose and capacity is directly correlated with student engagement and outcomes.

What's the Deal?

We reject the premise of robotic, standoffish and impersonal interactions with students in the classroom. We have observed some teachers who have adopted the "Don't smile till November" strategy. These teachers are under the impression that smiling in the classroom denotes a sign of weakness. As previously mentioned, in many cases, these teachers are given this advice by veteran teachers who may be a bit burned out or have come up with these strategies on their own merit. We are in agreement with the school of thought that says smiling and showing empathy are a crucial characteristic for a healthy classroom environment. More recently, Simonsen, Fairbanks, Briesch, Myers and Sugai (2008) have made the case for using evidence based practices as classroom management strategies. John and I will discuss these later in the chapter and in the MC notes.

Educators have long been concerned with student learning outcomes and student engagement in a classroom setting. Moreover, scholars have posited that both are affected by far more than just what happens in the classroom (Ladson-Billings, 1995; Mahiri, 2001; Peters, 2012; Travis, 2013). Simonsen et al. (2008) suggest that evidence of effective teachers cited from the 1960's and 1970's was not necessarily evidence based and could be the catalysts for many of these types of practices. However, more recent empirical evidence supports that learning outcomes and engagement are directly correlated with care and relationships exhibited by the teacher (Aspelin, 2010). In addition, we declare care and relationships can also have a positive effect classroom behavior management.

In the following section, we make the case for using popular culture and Discourse, whole-child development as precepts for relational pedagogy and care. With a goal of allowing students to have a voice, we believe that teachers can have a positive classroom management experience using relational pedagogy and care in their classrooms.

What's the Science?

So what's the science? The science is applying a pedagogy of youth culture. Youth culture theory supports many of the previously discussed tenets including relational pedagogy, care and hip-hop based education. We ultimately believe that the culmination of these strategies is a whole-child based education philosophy which teachers are morally obligated to uphold. Although we have spoken at length about HHBE, we will now take a moment to dig into the background on two important theoretical constructs which help shape YCP. Relational pedagogy describes a practice of teaching that places more importance on the relationship between the teacher and student rather than the behavior of the student. Essentially, Relational pedagogy dictates that behavior will be less of an obtrusive issue once strong, positive relationships are built and maintained. While care ethics underscores the importance of genuinely caring for another human being. When you apply this idea to teaching, it implies that educators should care for students because they are human beings first and foremost.

Relational Pedagogy

Aspelin (2011) states that teacher-student relationships are not only important for understanding student achievement, but is the foundation for inspiring student performance. Ladson-Billings (1995b) maintains that developing culturally relevant techniques are essential for student learning in urban settings. She emphasizes that "fluid relationships" between teachers and students extend beyond the classroom and into the community adding value to students' lives and the community as a whole. More research by Milner (2011) reinforces this idea and even takes it a step further, adding that teachers using a family approach plants seeds that go far beyond the classroom. By establishing these meaningful relationships, Milner (2011) asserts that teachers are essentially fighting for students' lives" and in doing so, care for the whole child (p. 86). For many years, scholars have also advocated caring for the whole child and involving the community in the learning process to improve student learning and engagement (Dewey, 1897; Epstein, 2011; Sanders & Lewis, 2005). As Ladson-Billings (1995) and Milner (2011) indicate, the benefits of teachers building relationships or rapport with students go far beyond the classroom. The relationship between the teacher and student stems from the teachers' desire to build a bond with the student. This relationship building encompasses a philosophy of educators acting to develop the whole-child through the pedagogy of relation (Sidorkin, 2000).

We feel that the construct of pedagogy of relation or relational pedagogy as explained by Sidorkin (2002) is pivotal to our approach at teaching. Sidorkin (2000) defines his pedagogy of relation as a description of a group or pair of people, "who interpret each other's words and actions through a certain prism of past experiences and culturally and socially induced expectations" (Sidorkin, 2000, p. 3). Aspelin (2011) extends Sidorkin's (2002) work adding to the scope of understanding and as such, we will use his definition of relational pedagogy. Aspelin (2011) defines relational pedagogy as a "theoretical discourse based on the notion of relationships as the basic unit of education"

(p. 10). To illustrate the journey of relational pedagogy, one must first look at educational discourse.

The general notion of educational discourse has taken two distinct paths. The first educational model, which Aspelin (2011) calls "the knowledge effective school," focuses on the academic achievement of the individual student (p. 6). Students' level of knowledge is assessed, tested and evaluated in order to place rank among classmates and ultimately, peers from other countries. In this model, more attention is paid to each student's extrinsic motivation and individual behavior (Sidorkin, 2000). This approach also aims to produce high-functioning, autonomous individuals who can perform well as a member of society. A second model, "the socially oriented school," focuses on the environment around the school. In this model, group processes and socio-cultural backgrounds are the focus (Aspelin, 2011, p. 6). The aim of this model is to ensure that students are socialized and able to be positive contributors to society (Aspelin, 2011). In search for an alternative, Aspelin (2011) sums up that relational pedagogy "ought to search for a path between a purely individualistic and a purely social understanding for education" (p. 6).

Sidorkin (2000) describes this pedagogy of relation as building relationships more so than constructing behaviors in students while focusing on a holistic and even spiritual approach to education. Sidorkin's work is reinforced by the work of Smyth (2006) who referred to this approach as "working to make students into powerful people" (p. 4). He clarified this as meaning the ability of teachers to make students feel empowered to accomplish tasks that may not have seem achievable before. Pearce and Down (2011) also support this premise affirming that positive relationships between teacher and student enable students to remain engaged. These scholars place relationships at the center of the schooling experience. Smyth (2006) explains further stating when relationships are not stressed, student engagement decreases and learning objectives are not attained.

In order to build relationships with students, teachers should meet students at their level (Emdin, 2009). By meeting them at their level, we mean that teachers should work to enhance students' current knowledge using prior knowledge that students may already have. One possible way to employ this technique is tapping into the popular culture in which most students are involved (Emdin, 2009; Petchauer, 2009). Scholars insist that educators pull elements from popular culture in order to reach students on a critical pedagogical level (Giroux, 1989; Mahiri, 2001; Morell, 2002; Duncan-Andrade, 2004; Bertonneau, 2010). Popular culture of today includes many of the entities students interact with on a daily basis such as television, social media and music. In fact, Mahiri (2001), uses the term popular culture pedagogy to include "TV, the internet, video games, music …, and movies" to help shape instruction in the classroom (p. 382). He further explains that these "modes of transmission" allow young people to evade limits on learning and meaning because of the familiarity (Mahiri, 2001, p. 382).

Additionally, the work of Gee (2003) also supports the idea of using popular culture, to inform the way that teachers educate. Gee (2003) declares that Discourse among social groups involving behavior, fashion and perspectives among other characteristics, can lead to further understanding when working with students. Using literacy, he lays out tenets that characterize how learning is not a separate function of our lives. However, the researcher is concerned with Gee's (2003) focus on the concept of how students learn with regards to his tenets. There are three tenets that deal with learning. Gee (2003) says that (1) learning can occur both in formal and informal contexts, (2) learning is a social process and finally, learning is grounded in historical precedence that shapes our ideas. These tenets directly align to meeting students at their level. They also support the idea that teachers should find out about their students' interests and experiences in order to become more effective teachers, thereby increasing student engagement (Compton-Lilly, 2007; Gee, 2003). Thus, using popular culture as a means to tap into what students already know and link it into something that they need to know, may possibly increase student engagement and learning outcomes.

Care Ethics

Although we have touched on it briefly in previous chapters, care ethics is sometimes viewed as a moral obligation rather than theory. The vast amount of research on care stems from some of the most ancient concepts of Confucian and African Ethics (Sander-Staudt, 2011). One of the more recent platforms on care was Mayeroff's (1972) theory that caring for others was an extension of caring for oneself. He upheld that care involves preserving the realm of others and meeting the needs of others and ourselves. Beginning in the 80's the ethic of care has been grounded in a framework of feminism as advanced by authors such as Gilligan (1993), Held (2005), Martin (1995) and Noddings (1984). These authors advance an ethic of care as the foundation of ethical decision making and the most basic moral theory with respect to politics, global and personal reasoning. Gilligan (1993) was perhaps one of the scholars who greatly advanced the ethic of care movement, claiming that society too often takes the male viewpoint on moral reasoning with no regard for the female voice. Noddings (2002) further developed the idea of care as a feminist ethic and suggested its place within moral education.

We will focus on the ethic of care as described by Noddings (2002) and use her definition of care. She explains that care can be broken down into two concepts; natural caring (a moral attitude that does not require an ethical stance to motivate it) and ethical caring (which is "rooted in receptivity, relatedness, and responsiveness") (p. 2). She further explains that in order for one to have care, three items must occur: First, receptive attention, meaning that the carer listens to what the cared for wants. In other words, there is a cyclical relationship in which the person caring hears the voice of the person being cared for. Second, the person being cared for must be receptive to and acknowledge the caring action. Finally, Noddings (2002) suggests that both parties must gain from the encounter.

Through Noddings (2002) work, we learn to care about others from our experiences of being cared for. Sidorkin (2002) tells us that relationships should be at the center of pedagogy. The two ideas align well when combined with a cultural pedagogical approach to teaching. Care generally must come from within the carer and out to the cared for (Noddings, 2002). Moreover, care is a relational act, geared toward the protection and well-being of the cared for (Gordon, Benner & Noddings, 1996). Noddings (2002) expands these ideas further and posits that "caring starts at home and moves outward until we learn to care about those we cannot care for directly" (p. 31). According to Noddings (2002) the caring that we learned from a young age becomes a part of who we are as people. She suggests that "caring about" adds to our sense of social justice and therefore our sense of social capital is eventually strengthened as a result.

YCP, when nestled within framework of relational pedagogy, care ethics and HHBE, allows students to have a voice in the classroom and gives teachers an upper hand at classroom management by not making behavior the focus. With a focus on relational strategies rather than behavioral strategies, in most instances, classroom management is something that doesn't cause as much anxiety for a teacher or the students.

MC Notes!

The first time I heard someone say the phrase "Don't Smile Until November" was in the teachers' lounge of the junior high school in which I was teaching.

Initially, I thought it was a joke, but as the teachers continued to talk about it, I began to see this was a real thing. It stuck with me so much I had to find out more. I began doing some research online and I learned that "Don't Smile until Christmas" was originally something that was shared in new teacher trainings to encourage new educators to begin their school year with a very strict and stern demeanor to keep their students under control. This would enable them to establish themselves as an authority figure in the early part of the school year. Basically, this was a classroom management technique that was designed to assure that classroom teachers got respect from their students in order to manage the classroom better.

After doing even more research, both online, as well as over the phone speaking directly with other educators in my network; I came across a blog post by Matthew R. Morris who is an elementary school educator, speaker, blogger and Anti-Racism Activist in Toronto, Canada. Morris's blog post entitled "Don't Smile until November" really resonated with me. It definitely inspired this song and chapter because I feel that doing the complete opposite of this concept is what leads to the best classroom management scenarios. A teacher that does not have a relationship with her students is one of the main sentiments that contribute to this idea of disconnected students and teachers across the globe. Without any real connection, there is no real learning happening, especially in an urban school setting. I witnessed the, so called, most troubled students become the most brilliant students once they felt safe in the classroom. I also witnessed many teachers not greeting their students when they entered the class. Instead, as they walked in the room, teachers would instruct them to start the "Bell Ringer" or copy the essential question on the board immediately like they were addressing robots instead of people. Imagine if these same teachers took the time to create safe spaces in the classroom that made the students feel welcome and valuable? There are many ways to make this happen.

Introduce Yourself to Your Class

One of the things I learned early in my teaching artist training was as follows: Before going into any formal instruction in a new class, be sure to introduce myself to the class beyond just my name and where I am from. I also discovered that it was important to learn about the students in that same way. I shared things about myself both verbally and visually allowing the students to understand that I had a life outside of the classroom just like they do. I am a hip-hop artist and entrepreneur and have been making/releasing music and traveling the world performing for the past 20 years; I usually start there. I bring in video clips of my live shows, radio interviews and music videos from different places in the world and even physical copies of my various CD and Vinyl releases for them to see and pass around the class. I recently got married so I show my wedding picture to the class and I even "spit" lyrics or perform a song to let them know it's real. Doing this is helpful with getting students to feel comfortable and share more about who they are as people.

Starburst Game

A great activity I use to get to know new students in a fun way, I call the "Starburst Game." In this activity you can use Starburst or any candy that comes in a variety of colors such as Skittles and Jolly Ranchers. First make a key that connects the colors of the candy to questions relating to the students that they will answer later in the game. Once the key is up and can be seen by the entire class, walk around the classroom asking each student to take 3 pieces of candy only. Be sure to let the students know that if they eat their candy before we start the game just hold on to the wrappers to remember the colors they picked. The object is to now go around the room encouraging students to share their responses based on the questions connected to the colors of the candy they chose.

Each time I do this not only do I learn a lot about the students in the classroom but they also learn so much more about each other and this always serves as a great community building activity. To be fair I'm sure the candy helps a little bit too LOL!

Whenever I meet new students in the beginning of the school year I'm always mindful of the fact the students don't know me yet and it is important to break the ice with topics and activities they will resonate with and be excited about. In these activities, I usually ask them about their favorite songs, albums, music artists, movies, TV shows, places in the world to visit, sports teams, social media platforms and other youth culture based magic that would be embraced in a 21st century urban school setting. In my experience taking this approach always shows the students that I care about the things that are important to them and even when I wasn't spot on they always show appreciation for my willingness to try to understand. Building community in a classroom is not something that magically happens overnight. It is imperative to respect the process and one of the most potent ingredients for me is consistency. The real magic begins to happen once I am able to learn directly from the students and activate that learning by bringing in materials they relate to.

I also try to consistently create a safe space where their voices and perspective are valued the most.

Other Introductory Games

Games certainly seem to work best when working with students. Many teachers ask us for ideas and feel like games are the easiest. So we have decided to include a few games to help educators get to know their students and vice versa.

Scavenger Hunt

This is a game that the teacher prepares beforehand, quite possibly hiding artifacts around the classroom. Students can be asked various questions about the room, the school, principal, teachers etc. I also add demographic information on the sheet as well such as parent or guardian's name and their phone number or email. It is also useful for asking questions about the student to get to know them. It is a great way to get students up and moving around and talking. When completed, go over the sheet with the class.

Who Are You—Bingo and Jeopardy

Those who have been teaching for a while are probably familiar with using bingo or Jeopardy in the classroom. I too was handed these ideas from other teachers. I generally play this game once I have started getting to know my students. Although these games are generally used to review material for understanding or for a test, these games are also good to get to know students in a greater capacity. For instance, once I know that the class is generally interested in a particular topic, I use these games to find out how much they know about a topic concerning popular or youth culture. Using a regular bingo board, I use this to find out different things students are into. I have squares with answers like Swim, skateboard, surf the internet, listen to different types of music, etc. Jeopardy is very similar. I use Microsoft Excel to create a jeopardy board with categories on hip-hop or skateboarding or video games (depending on which activities my students seem to be into the most). These games are great catalysts to conversations and can even be used to introduce or study guide review a topic later in the semester. (See YCP Activity Guide for more detailed descriptions).

Move Away from Teacher vs Student Mindset

I truly feel that without taking the time to build up a genuine solid relationship with your students, classroom management and all other communication with your students becomes the most difficult part of one's career as an educator. I never feel like "They don't have to like me but they better respect me," without a true connection there is no respect and usually leads to unproductive sessions in class every week. My goal is always to move away from the Teacher vs. Student mind set which places the teacher in the center of the classroom as an authority figure. Teachers should allow students to be in the driver's seat of what is happening in class to assure that we are being productive and their voices and contributions are being heard and valued. I never yell at students because when I see other teachers yelling at the students it never gets them the results for which they are looking. I understand that some of our students get yelled at all the time and witness so many harsh realities in their lives outside of school and online that they are desensitized from violence or being treated negatively. I am more focused on seeing how much differently the students act when I treat them with respect and care and let them know that their ideas and concerns are important to me.

The biggest challenge for me has always been not having enough face time with students to be able to build these relationships sooner and more solidly. As a teaching artist, I see each of my middle school classes twice a week and my high school classes three to five times a week. The difficult part of being in the classroom in the beginning was feeling like I was starting over every week. This type of schedule makes it difficult to build solid relationships with the students in a way that allows a trust and respect for each other to grow organically. Despite the limitations, I am still successful at connecting and nurturing student relationships and creating safe spaces in classrooms where students feel comfortable expressing themselves and learning. Many of the students I've worked with over the past six years in New York City public schools don't know what it feels like to be revered in a classroom based on who they are. After speaking with and getting to know a lot of these students over the years, I learned that many of the students have mostly had negative and traumatic situations with teachers and other school staff.

Using Youth Culture in Your Daily Lessons

However if you are teaching from the perspective of youth culture and the students are now able to see themselves in the work, then things can change drastically. Whenever we create art in class based on the lesson plan, the process of creating the art helps students remember their lessons. The art created in class

can be, but not limited to, poems, raps, songs, hooks, memes, hash tags, draw-
ings, vision boards, a processed drama skit re-enacting a historical event or part
of a book and more. I have witnessed on so many occasions students who were
totally tuned out and not interested in learning. However, once they are able
to objectify the experience with a creative process, these same students soon
became leaders in the classroom. They were creating art based on the subjects
being taught. But they were using their gifts to create, which allowed them to
embody the lessons instead of just memorizing it. Many students are also well
versed in the latest happenings in youth culture and therefore are able to contribute more to class and eventually feel more confident and comfortable participating in class in general. I love the fact that now when students see me they
already think that something innovative and different is going to happen in
class today. This developed from consistently catering to their cultural palettes
by letting youth culture, and specifically their own ideas, drive the lesson plans
and activities. It also feels good to walk in school and stroll down the hall and
always get love from the students in the form of peace signs, salutes, fist bumps
and handshakes. These relationships were nurtured by always showing them
love and also showing them that I genuinely care about their well-being. Of
course being consistent in these sentiments is important.

Through this journey I learned that teaching is a love sport. To enjoy
it you have to enjoy young people and be open minded and willing to see
through their lenses as it relates to hip-hop and youth culture, even if you
don't understand it at first. The love is shown by your intentions. Students can
easily see right through something that isn't genuine and without that simple
trust we are missing an entire generation of students.

Something else I would like to share that I started doing and it grew to
be a great way to build relationships with my students while outside of class. I
began to send videos from different places in the world I was visiting for performances to my co-teachers and subs to play in class for the students during
my absence. One of the huge perks of being a teaching artist in NYC is that
I can still travel with my creative career due to having access to a network of
skilled teaching artist that can sub my class with my plans and materials that I
planned together with my co-teacher. Due to this I have been fortunate over
the past few years while teaching to travel to places like Austria, Germany,
France, Japan, Australia and other places in the U.S. and many of these places
I made videos showing the students where I was in the world. I let the students
know that I was thinking about them and encourage them to stay focused
and have a great week, the goal is to have a positive exchange that doesn't

traditionally happen in school. I never miss more than a week of class during these trips to keep good standing with all parties involved. Ever since sending the first video from a far I was able to see how much the students embraced and appreciated that gesture and also learned how it sparked their curiosity with all the questions they had for me about these different places. Taking this approach has given me positive results so far and also allowed me to grow aspirations of travel and creative entrepreneurialism in the minds and hearts of the students. My method is mainly keeping an open heart and mind toward young people and the various cultural esthetics they champion and live by. Care and genuine intentions matter more than anything, without either of these that true connection never happens. Keep Smiling.

Audi 5000

So are you one of the teachers who don't smile until November? Does a using robotic, standoffish and impersonal interaction with students really work for you? We are willing to bet that it does not. Is change possible? Yes but it really depends on you. Are you in it for yourself or for your students?

For educators, changing involves shifting of the current mindset; reversing the current trend. Relational pedagogy offers a fresh approach to education in which children, and not data, are the center of the educational sphere. According to our research, switching to a mindset of relational pedagogy not only allows teachers to express care, which these students need, but it generally lowers discipline issues. Of course, we invite more studies of this idea, but for the last decade, we have used this approach with great success. We do believe that the behaviorist mentality is archaic and does not work with new century students. They are far too sophisticated to just accept what is given to them. For our generation and the generation before us, the old adage "do it because I said so" seemed to go work. However, any teacher, administrator or parent can attest to the fact that this saying does not work as easy as it used to. These students don't accept the "do it because I said so" ideology. They are far too technologically savvy to not Google the how and the why. Let's discuss some of these differences.

Interlude 2: Free

"Serving up the mystery meat, it's all FREE FREE, Murder Burgers & Suicide Fries for the FREE FREE The Lowest Grades of Meats and Dairy that's FREE FREE, It's hard to pay attention, Man I'm getting sleepy!"

Free Free was directly inspired by my public school experience growing up in New York City. I can remember if you were given a free lunch ticket, it meant that your family didn't make a certain amount of money and therefore you were given either free or reduced lunch while other kids had to pay for their lunch every day. Although I never voiced it until now, it was pretty humiliating getting teased by other students because I got free lunch. Even though we ate it we always complained about it. The burgers never looked like meat. The fries were always soggy and under cooked. The fruit and green vegetables were little or next to none. The food was cold and I could go on for days.

Just think, going to the cafeteria after gym the last thing we ever needed was a box of chocolate milk to quench our thirst, SMH. As I reflect back on my experience, I can't help but think, "Where was the water?" "Did they ever serve fruits and vegetables?" The answer is if they did then why couldn't I remember that happening? Clearly it wasn't enough. As I fast forward to today, I am still hearing these same exact conversations from students in both middle and high school. Most of the same exact complaints from when I was in school are still around today. I hear the students talk about how the meats don't look real. I talk to students who compare the food, lunchroom set up and entire school lunch experience to how prison cafeterias are shown on television and in films.

I witnessed students coming to 6th period right after lunch and they would be bouncing off the walls. This is because they didn't have recess and their entire lunch consisted of sugar and starch which made them very hyper in the beginning of class. By time they got to 7th period they were sleepy and didn't have the energy they should as youngsters. These instances made me start to think about how the limited information about nutrition and healthy food in black and brown communities are affecting our children. When asked, some students in the 8th grade and some in high school didn't truly know what a balanced meal should look like or what healthy food options are. I am not a health guru, a doctor or a nutritionist, but I couldn't help but think about how these limited food choices offered in school are negatively affecting our young people. Being an optimistic thinker most of the time, I would the immediately begin thinking "what if students were offered healthy, wholesome, nutritionally balanced lunches that they enjoyed?" How much would this change their school day and overall ability to focus and learn? How long are we going to start our youth 20 steps behind the rest of the world but expect excellence in return?

Free Free is a call to educators and administrators to ask that you all consider what the students are eating every day and how it could be a major part of other issues happening in school such as hyperactivity and falling asleep. Free Free is a call to parents to pay closer attention to what your children are eating at home and in school and how during this impressionable time in their lives these habits may dictate how they understand nutrition as an adult. Free Free is a reminder that our children deserve a fair chance just like everyone else in the world and let's start by at the very least ensuring they are being provided a quality balanced meal during their school day so that they may focus and be their best self each and every day.

References

Appiah, K. A. (2007). *Cosmopolitanism: Ethics in a world of strangers* (Issues of our time). New York, NY: W.W. Norton & Company.

Aspelin, J. (2010). What really matters is 'between': Understanding the focal point of education from an inter-human perspective. *Education Inquiry, 1*(2), 127–136.

Aspelin, J. (2011). Co-existence and co-operation: the two-dimensional conception of education. *Education, 1*(1), 6–11.

Bertonneau, T. F. (2010). A counter-curriculum for the pop culture classroom. *Academic Questions, 23*(4), 420–434.

Canter, L. (1989). Assertive discipline: More than names on the board and marbles in a jar. *The Phi Delta Kappan, 71*(1), 57–61.

Compton-Lilly, C. (2007). What can video games teach us about teaching reading? *Reading Teacher, 60*, 718–727.

Dewey, J. (1897). My pedagogic creed. *School Journal.* Washington, DC: Progressive Education Association.

Duncan-Andrade, J. M. (2004). Your best friend or your worst enemy: youth popular culture, pedagogy, and curriculum in urban classrooms. *The Review of Education, Pedagogy and Cultural Studies, 26*, 313–337.

Emdin, C. (2009). Rethinking student participation: a model from hip-hop and urban science education. *Edge Phi Delta Kappa International, 5*(1), 1–18.

Epstein, J. L. (2011). *School, family, and community partnerships: Preparing educators and improving schools* (2nd edition). Boulder, CO: Westview Press.

Fullan, M. (2003). *The moral imperative of school leadership.* Toronto: Corwin.

Gee, J. P. (2003). *What video games have to teach us about learning and literacy.* New York, NY: Palgrave Macmillan.

Gilligan, C. (1993). *In a different voice: Psychological theory and women's development.* Cambridge, MA: Harvard University Press.

Giroux, H. A. (1989). *Schooling and the struggle for public life: Critical pedagogy in the modern age.* Minneapolis, MN: University of Minnesota Press.

Gordon, S., Benner, P., & Noddings, N. (Eds.). (1996). *Caregiving: Readings in knowledge, practice, ethics, and politics.* Philadelphia, PA: University of Pennsylvania Press.

Held, V. (2005). *The ethics of care: Personal, political, and global.* Oxford: Oxford University Press.

Ladson-Billings, G. (1995). Toward a theory of culturally relevant pedagogy. *American Educational Research Journal, 32*(3), 465–491.

Mahiri, J. (2001). Pop culture pedagogy and the end(s) of school. *Journal of Adolescent & Adult Literacy, 44*(4), 382–85.

Martin, J. R. (1995). *The schoolhome: Rethinking schools for changing families.* Cambridge, MA: Harvard University Press.

Martin, N., Yin, Z., & Mayall, H. (2006). Classroom management training, teaching experience and gender: Do these variables impact teachers' attitudes and beliefs toward classroom management. *The Annual Conference of Southwest Educational Research Association.* Austin, TX.

Mayeroff, M. (1972). *On caring* (Vol. 1971). Oxford: Harper Collins Publishers.

Miller, R. (1997). *What are schools for: Holistic education in American culture* (3rd ed.). Brandon, VT: Holistic Education Press.

Milner, H. R. (2011). Culturally relevant pedagogy in a diverse urban classroom. *Urban Review. 43,* 66–89.

Morrell, E. (2002). Toward a critical pedagogy of popular culture: Literacy development among urban youth. *Journal of Adolescent & Adult Literacy, 46(1),* 72–77.

Morris, M. (n.d.). Don't smile until November? [Web log post]. Retrieved from http://www.matthewrmorris.com/classroom-management/dont-smile-november/

Noddings, N. (1984). *Caring: A feminine approach to ethics and moral education.* Berkeley, CA: University of CA Press.

Noddings, N. (2002). *Educating moral people: A caring alternative to character education.* New York, NY: Teachers College Press.

Palmer, P. J. (2003). *To know as we are known: Education as a spiritual journey.* San Francisco, CA: Harper San Francisco.

Pearce, J., & Down, B. (2011) Relational pedagogy for student engagement and success at university. *The Australian Educational Researcher, 38*(4), 483–494.

Petchauer, E. (2009). Framing and reviewing hip-hop educational research. *Review of Educational Research, 79*(2), 946–978.

Peters, J. H. (2012). Are they ready? Final year pre-service teachers learning about managing student behaviour. *Australian Journal of Teacher Education, 37*(9), 17–42.

Redman, P. (2006). *Don't smile until December, and other myths about classroom teaching.* Thousand Oaks, CA: Corwin Press.

Sander-Staudt, M. (2011). Care ethics. Internet Encyclopedia of Philosophy.

Sanders, M. G., & Lewis, K. C. (2005). Building bridges toward excellence: Community involvement in high schools. *The High School Journal, 88*(3), pp. 1–9.

Sidorkin, A. M. (2000). *Toward a Pedagogy of Relation.* Retrieved from http://digitalcommons.ric.edu/facultypublications/17

Sidorkin, A. M. (2002). *Learning relations: Impure education, deschooled schools, and dialogue with evil*. New York, NY: Peter Lang.

Simonsen, B., Fairbanks, S., Briesch, A., Myers, D., & Sugai, G. (2008). Evidence-based practices in classroom management: Considerations for research to practice. *Education and Treatment of Children, 31*(1), 351–380.

Smyth, J. (2006). 'When students have power': student engagement, student voice, and the possibilities for school reform around 'dropping out' of school. *International Journal of Leadership in Education, 9*(4), 285–298.

Travis, R., Jr. (2013). Rap music and the empowerment of today's youth: Evidence in everyday music listening, music therapy, and commercial rap music. *Child and Adolescent Social Work Journal, 30*(2), 139–167.

· 4 ·

GENERATION XYZ

"Gen Z with the most know how of em all, so clever for sure, technological genius from the door"

Say What?

In order to speak about the generation of students that we are now teaching, we feel it's imperative that we attempt to define some parameters. In 2015, a marketing and branding company named Ologie completed a study on Generation Z ("This is Gen Z," 2015). In this study, they labeled the generations as follows:

Table 4.1

Group	Years Born
Generation X	1965–1979
Generation Y	1980–1995
Generation Z	1996–After

While we are aware that there are several interpretations of each group's birth years, these are the years we will use for our purposes. According to Strauss and Howe (1991) the generation born 1996 and after has been labeled by several names. Some have called them the iGeneration or iGen (based on the popularity of iPhones). The U.S. Department of Health and Human Services labeled them the Post-Millennial generation while a contest sponsored by USA Today came up with the suggestion of Generation Z (Strauss & Howe, 1991). The latter is what we will use for our description of the generation that follows Generation Y. This description also works with the title for our song "XYZ." While Berk (2009) explains that these specific dates, ages and labels can be left up to interpretation, these are the parameters that we will use to define the groups of which we speak throughout this chapter. Now let's define some of the important characteristics of Generation Z.

According to the Center for Generational Kinetics, in 2015 Generation Z was about 23% of the population of the United States (Villa & Dorsey, 2017). The breakdown on this is about 55% Caucasian, 24% Hispanic, 14% Black, 4% Asian and 4% other (Strauss, 1991). While 9/11 is a defining moment for Generation Y, Generation Z barely remembers these attacks. According to the parameters that we are using, members of Generation Z were small children during 9/11. It is a history lesson for them. This generation also does not remember a time without smartphones (Gibson, Cabler, Cance, Beck & Santos, 2013). Strauss (1991) points out that 75% of Generation Z use smartphones more than they watch TV. In fact, Palfrey and Gasser (2016) calls this generation "Digital Natives," explaining that they are more comfortable with digital media than any generation before them. They are so comfortable with using digital technology that they use the internet for almost all communications with family and friends.

For this group, social media is the most important means of communication. According to CaptureHigherEd.com Generation Z is all about mobile technology ('What's App with Gen Z?," 2017). They value their internet connection more than most activities such as going to the movies or having cable TV ('What's App with Gen Z?," 2017). They value SnapChat, YouTube and Instagram and consider Facebook and Twitter for 'old people' (Villa & Dorsey, 2017). Applications that give them anonymity, use less personal information and that are "more instantaneous" are more appealing to this group. They are used to clicking the 'like' button and are more likely to trust a friend's endorsement rather than an advertiser's endorsement (Gibson et al., 2013). This is also a technically smarter generation than their predecessors. Villa and Dorsey (2017) elaborate on the fact that their tech savvy ways mean that they approach problem solving in a different way than generations before them.

All these characteristics are important for educators to keep in mind. Strauss (1991) explains that members of Generation Z are primarily the children of Generation X. This is an important distinction that we will touch on later.

So, what are some of the implications of these characteristics? Let's start with the fact that Generation Z is considered to be the digital generation. Moreover, they generally don't remember a time before social media. So, it makes sense that they live a majority of their lives in an online, virtual world. They prefer to communicate with pictures and videos rather than writing or even a phone call. All these factors have huge implications on how Generation Z learns, trains and even problem solves. Why shouldn't we as educators reach these students on this platform in which they are already immersed? How can we use these common characteristics to reach these students where they are?

What's the Deal?

In our song 'XYZ', we give you a glimpse into what we have seen as educators. Many times, we have seen teachers and administrators fight an uphill battle to ban everything that is important to Generation Z. Current behavioristic methods are focusing on items such as headphones and cell phones. When you walk into a classroom the first sign or rule you will see is "NO CELL PHONES." We have observed this from Brooklyn to Columbus in many classrooms and schools. Students are told to put their headphones in their lockers and to stay off of social media during school hours. This seems fair to us as members of Generation X. However, if you prescribe to the characteristics described in the preceding section, then this would make school a very difficult place for you to thrive. We understand that technology is at the core of Generation Z student's world. The "No Cell Phones" policy of our generation is not working. With this in mind, we must stop fighting this technology and commit to finding ways to embrace it and use to help us reach these students. The current 'No Cell Phones' policy is dividing the teachers and student population.

Instead, we propose embracing technology and creating complimentary material and pedagogy with which to use it in the classroom. Subsequently, using the prior knowledge of our students aligns with culturally relevant pedagogy (Ladson-Billings, 1995). Further, understanding the culture of the youth pushes forward the previously mentioned concept of culturally sustaining pedagogy and makes a case for youth culture pedagogy as the next wave (Ladson-Billings, 2014; Paris, 2012; Paris & Alim, 2014). With these thoughts in mind, let's discuss in detail those implications for education that we mentioned earlier.

Things to Keep in Mind with Generation Z Students

Generation Z students are already technologically savvy. They grew up in a digital world in which mobile technology has always been prominent. They expect information to always be at their fingertips. Moreover, they are used to things moving at a fast pace and can generally keep up with technological advancements more so than the generations before them. About 89% of these students use google to search for information as they have an ease-of-use" mentality (Berk, 2009, p. 9). They have never used an encyclopedia and as such don't quite see plagiarism or copying information down as inherently 'wrong'. According to Ladson-Billings, they live in a culture that is a mash-up, everything in their lives is a sample (UMH Hurley Convergence Center, 2017). Subsequently, real and virtual can sometimes be intertwined in their world. As educators of these Gen Z students, we must make adjustments that fit with how they use technology on an everyday basis.

In addition, one of the most important distinctions with Generation Z and other generations before them is they are not only consumers of internet content at a young age, but they are also some of the greatest contributors to that content. Berk (2009) explains that many of them design websites, post to blogs and create original artwork and pictures for internet consumption. Consequently, this also makes them used to instant gratification. I refer to them as the "micro-wave generation." They expect everything to happen in a quick and equally responsive manner. This in turn, makes things get "old" to them much more quickly. For instance, the span of an album doesn't last as long as it used to. With a decreased attention span, multi-tasking seems to work best for this generation. Things in their environment need to move quickly and when it does not, they become bored with it. Again, as educators of these Gen Z students, we should harness this creativity to create new ways for our students to discover, analyze and evaluate using higher order thinking skills.

Berk (2009) also explains that on a whole, this generation would rather learn by doing and by trial and error. They enjoy being engaged and constantly connected (Berk, 2009; UMH Hurley Convergence Center, 2017). They would also communicate visually. This is why YouTube and Snap-Chat are current favorites. Social interaction and face-to-face encounters are important in their lives which could possibly make teamwork a preferred method of interactions (Berk, 2009).

Research on Generation Z

According to Villa and Dorsey (2017), there has been very little empirical educational research to discover the mindset, habits, behaviors and priorities Generation Z. The bulk of the research that has been conducted has been overseen by marketing and branding companies who seek to discover this information in order to establish better ways to market and sell to this generation. Colleges are among the foremost interested recipients of this information. They are interested in finding ways to market their university to this new generation of future college students. According to one of these research companies, "brands and employers will have to learn how to see the world through the diverse eyes of Generation Z if they want to win their loyalty" ('What's App with Gen Z?," 2017, p. 1).

Why aren't we as educators working as hard as the marketing companies to see the world through Generation Z's eyes? If we want to educate them doesn't it make sense that we would want to win their loyalty as well? How can you educate someone that you haven't taken the time to get to know or understand? YCP seeks to answer these questions, but with the understanding of using youth culture such as hip-hop as the catalyst.

What's the Science?

So, what's the science? The science is applying a pedagogy of youth culture. We believe that just as these marketing and branding companies are studying the culture of this generation to gain an understanding of their buying habits, educators should be studying the culture of this generation in order to better teach them. The next step is to apply these characteristics we learned about Generation Z from the marketing and branding companies to our educational practices. We are interested in discovering how we can improve student engagement and relationships using what we know about this generation's behaviors, habits and culture to help gain insight to teaching them. We think that using youth culture (and in this case, hip-hop) as a starting point will allow educators to gain these valuable insights. The next section will explore ways in which Gen X educators can connect with Gen Z students and how YCP can play a pivotal role in building this connection.

Hip-hop as a Tool for Transaction

We feel that hip-hop culture is a great entry point for an educator to try to get to know his or her students. In many cases, students will identify with hip-hop culture in some aspect. One important point to consider is the point that in many cases, members of Gen Z and Gen X generally enjoy the same music, hip-hop. As our friend and colleague, DJ O Sharp, pointed out, this may be the first time in many years that parents and children enjoy the same culture, style and type of music. As we alluded to earlier, this is an important distinction because it is a possible starting point for conversation between parent and child or even teacher and student. And as we have practiced many times, it can be a great segue into gaining an understanding and even building a relationship with a student. It has implications for members of Gen X who consider themselves members of the hip-hop generation. But it also has important implications for members of Gen X who do NOT consider themselves members of the hip-hop generation.

For members of the hip-hop generation who grew up on artists like Rakim, KRS-One and Nas; we KNOW hip-hop. However, let's take a step back. We KNOW our hip-hop. Hip-hop is ever changing. In reality, any culture evolves and changes. So let's keep it real, we may know our hip-hop, but maybe we don't know much about our students' hip-hop. True, we know the culture. We understand why "freaking your sneakers" is important. We actually understand why it's cool to have a little sag in your pants. However, we don't always necessarily "get" the new style of hip-hop of today's youth. Dubbed "mumble rap" because sometimes the auto tune laden words are difficult to understand, today's hip-hop has a different sound then the classic boom-bap era that many Gen X'ers are used to. However, I implore you, hip-hop members of the Gen X generation, not to give up on today's hip-hop youth.

Think back to a time when you were just discovering hip-hop. Older generations (probably Baby boomers) probably told you that your music was "just noise" and "wouldn't last." Now all these years later, it's still here. It's just different. You may even feel the same way about today's hip-hop. But it's still hip-hop. We think this is important to keep in mind when working with Gen Z students. If you grew up in the Golden Era of hip-hop, use your knowledge of hip-hop to inform your inquiry into their new style of hip-hop. Ask them who is their favorite emcee or favorite producer. Have them explain to you why they like those artists. Have frank discussions about their favorites compared to your favorites. This could be a great opportunity for rich thick discussion in an academic setting. In the meantime, through these discussions, you are learning more about the student. In fact, you are building a positive relation-ship with the student at the same time.

Conversely, for educators who do NOT identify with the hip-hop gener-ation, the same principle applies to you as well. The main difference is that you will ask the student questions about hip-hop in a genuine attempt to learn more. Even if you have a small idea about hip-hop, allowing the student the opportunity to inform and teach you, the teacher, about hip-hop builds their confidence, competence and your relationship. Ask the students ques-tions about the culture. Ask them questions about their favorite artists and to defend their opinion on them. Find out ways you can create opportunities for transaction between you and your students.

YCP is at the forefront of the above examples. Most importantly, in these instances, you are following Sidorkin's (2002) idea of polyphonic authority by allowing the student to teach you about hip-hop. Additionally, while you learn about hip-hop or the type of hip-hop that your students enjoy, there is a transaction occurring within the classroom (Elon University, 2012). By tak-ing the time to learn about something that is important to you students, they also understand that you care about them (Noddings, 2002). Consequently, this approach allows a teacher to learn about their students' cultural identities and to use this information for lesson planning and connecting with students.

MC Notes!

In light of many of the challenges facing parents raising children in a fast-paced technologically advanced world, we thought it prudent to add another element of engagement that could empower both parents and educators. Although often understated, the connection between teachers, administra-tors and parents is of the utmost importance to the development students. Connections developed from a strong alliance between parents and school administrators are invaluable to the success of our students. The Power of Per-formance activity is one that we use to build a sense of family with educators and parents. This is a chance for a principal or teacher to step out of comfort zone and engage with parents in activities that are outside the school norms. We see this as a community building effort that is left field to normal school culture. At the end of the day it's using hip hop culture and aesthetics to implement community building in a way that teachers, parents and adminis-trators can enjoy and have fun doing. When students see them in an activity that shows them actually enjoying each other, it sends a powerful message.

The Power of Performance

In this workshop, parents, teachers and students will engage in various activities and a discussion about the power of performance and how it can enhance
a student's social skills and also school practices. The goal of the workshop is
to share a greater understanding of how performing within the arts (whether
it is rapping, singing, dancing, poetry, theater or any other art forms) lend to
skills that can empower students in their school careers or life in general. This
is an activity, which can be used with parents and educators. It can also be
used by a teacher who needs to 'break the ice' with her class. What follows are
three main points about the power of performance.

Students that feel confident about performing their art form are more
likely to:

1. Participate and Present work in class
2. Socialize in school (Lunch Time, Gym and Recess)
3. Communicate and express themselves more effectively.

Hype Man

Greet participants: WELCOME EVERYONE, THANKS FOR BEING HERE

1. Everyone choose a partner from the audience that you either don't
   know that well or don't know at all.
2. Spend two minutes talking to learn more about them. At the end of 2
   minutes you will switch

Call and Response

Call and response is a form of interaction between a speaker and an audience
in which the speaker's statements ("calls") are punctuated by responses from
the listeners (Audience).

Fill in the Blanks

The game is played with one volunteer playing the role of the guesser who
will - FILL IN THE BLANKS and another volunteer is in the role of giving
the clues. The object of the activity is for the sitting volunteer to guess a series
of words based on descriptions given to them by the freestyler. The only twist

is you must freestyle rap the descriptions in order for your partner to guess the correct words.

Audi 5000

What can you do to learn more about Gen Z? As a teacher, administrator or parent, is it your responsibility to find out what makes them tick or is it the other way around? For us, the answer is simple. Whether you are Gen X or Gen Y, it's up to you to find out about the students that you teach. For teachers, XYZ is about remembering when you were young. Remember how you felt when someone allowed you to express an interest. Whether your students are into rock music, video games, or ice hockey; YCP explains that we can use that to open a window into their world. This is why our ideas align with hip-hop education so well. Many of the students in urban areas are naturally a part of the hip-hop generation. And since hip-hop culture and pop culture now are synonymous, the use of #HipHopEd has far reaching effects from urban to suburban and even some rural communities.

This is not an easy task. Let's be honest, hip-hop then and now are different. Some Gen X hip-hop fans are not particularly fans of the path that hip-hop has taken. And for someone that is not familiar with hip-hop, the task of infusing hip-hop into pedagogy can seem challenging. However, the beauty of YCP with hip-hop education is actually in the challenge. It can be a challenge for the teacher or parent to give up a little authority. However, forging ahead with ideas like Hype-Man and Call and Response allow teachers to grow and learn as well. Using hip-hop in the classroom may not be for everyone, but it really depends on you. Are you in it for yourself or for your students?

References

Berk, R. (2009). Teaching strategies for the net generation. *Transformative Dialogues: Teaching & Learning Journal, 3*(2), 1–24.

[Elon University]. (2012, March 15). Christopher Emdin speaks to Elon teaching fellows [Video File]. Retrieved from https://www.youtube.com/watch?v=a9Ob2CRjh94

Gibson, K., Cabler, T., Cance, K., Beck, J., & Santos, J. (2013). Generation z: The next generation of college students, presented at NIRSA Inspiring Communities of Well-Being Conference, Las Vegas, 2013, Las Vegas, NV: NIRSA.

Ladson-Billings, G. (1995). But that's just good teaching! The case for culturally relevant pedagogy. *Theory into Practice, 34*(3), 159–165.

Ladson-Billings, G. (2014). Culturally relevant pedagogy 2.0 a.k.a. the remix. *Harvard Educational Review, 84*(1), 74–84.

Noddings, N. (2002). *Educating moral people: A caring alternative to character education*. New York, NY. Teachers College Press.

Palfrey, J., & Gasser, U. (2016). *Born digital: Understanding the first generation of digital natives*. New York, NY: Basic Books.

Paris, D. (2012). Culturally sustaining pedagogy: A needed change in stance, terminology, and practice. *Educational Researcher, 41*(3), 93–97.

Paris, D., & Alim, H. S. (2014). What are we seeking to sustain through culturally sustaining pedagogy? A loving critique forward. *Harvard Educational Review, 84*(1), 85–100.

Sidorkin, A. M. (2002). *Learning relations: Impure education, deschooled schools, and dialogue with evil*. New York, NY: Peter Lang.

Strauss, W., & Howe, N. (1991). *Generations*. New York, NY: Quill, William Morrow.

[UMH Hurley Convergence Center]. (2017, April 6). Dr. Gloria Ladson-Billings, "Hip hop, hip hope: Reinventing culturally relevant pedagogy" [Video File]. Retrieved from https://www.youtube.com/watch?v=oj4z6AQj9zA

Villa, D., & Dorsey, J. (2017). *Gen Z White Paper –The State of Gen Z 2017 National Research Study*. Retrieved from The Center for Generational Kinetics Website: https://genhq.com/gen-z-2017/

What's App with Gen Z? (2017). Retrieved from https://capturehighered.com/wp-content/uploads/2016/11/SocialMediaGenZ.pdf

· 5 ·

WE AIN'T FAILING

"And that's one reason why the students aren't winning; got standardized testing on individualized children …"

Say What?

According to Zitlow and Kohn (2001), standardized testing has several aims. Among some of those aims are the following: a means of promoting a sense of "back-to-basics instruction," for political gain and for corporate profits. Standardized testing in America has grown into its own business. For years teachers and students alike have complained about standardized testing; and for years standardized testing has remained the "go-to" method for measuring learning within our schools. In a survey conducted by Walker (2016) nearly seventy percent of teachers agreed that current standardized testing methods were an inefficient means of means of measurement. Limits of the testing include: not assessing material that students had the opportunity to learn during the school year, providing feedback to students to assist with learning, and assisting educators in setting responsible academic goals for students (Walker, 2016). We understand this issue to include many different forms of testing. For the ease of understanding, in this chapter, we will speak of standardized testing in terms of academic assessment.

An approach to assessment which incorporates student's prior knowledge is one possible solution. Teachers who allow students to inform learning in the classroom are offering an environment in which learning can flourish. When student prior knowledge is considered, students feel a sense of self-worth and communal attitude which can transform bad classrooms into meccas of learning and engagement. For instance, when the civilizations of a great empire such as the Aztecs are studied, there is a focus on their way of life. We study the nuances, intricacies and flaws to their way of life. We encompass their whole culture. Why do we not incorporate this philosophy into who we study with? Our students have a culture. They have a way of life. This youth culture should be celebrated and used as a primary focus with which to introduce new ideas, explore cultures of the past and to generate excitement for learning.

We have seen our classrooms flourish when we allow our students to inform the curriculum. We pose the following questions: Does testing and assessment need to be standardized? Our students are not standardized why should testing be? Our primary stance is that education is more relative and thus, assessment would need to fall into the same realm of thinking. We pronounce that the current testing structure is not flexible enough to be effective with our individualized students.

What's the Deal?

As previously mentioned, we have seen our students struggle with these standardized tests. We have witnessed our students giving into the notion that they are expected to be a standard deviation behind their white counterparts. This is a function of the current tracking system that has become customary within our educational system. We have also had to pick up the pieces when our students fail to graduate due to a standardized test. Such low expectations eventually become the norm and students begin to perform at these expected levels. According to Walpole, McDonough, Bauer, Gibson, Kanyi, and Toliver (2005), African-American and Latino students have traditionally underperformed on standardized college entrance exams. They also explain that, despite this fact, researchers have not been able to pinpoint the cause for this achievement gap (Walpole et al., 2005). We submit that the cause of this gap is directly aligned with the cultural biases represented within these exams. We have identified several key characteristics of these exams which augment these biases. First, these tests do not speak to the intelligence of marginalized youth. Second, the tests do not represent all aspects of the youth being tested.

Finally, since these youth do not see themselves in the messages represented by these tests, they begin to show signs of resentment toward school, educators and even the learning process.

First, we must look at how intelligence is defined at the school level. Winner (1997) explains that the term 'gifted' was used to describe students with a certain IQ score. The use of a standardized measuring process such as the IQ test set the standard for what would come to define intelligence. In recent years, many have chosen to adopt Gardner's (2011) theory of multiple intelligences as a guideline for basing intellect. Hatt (2007) argues that the way intelligence is calculated in our schools is destructive to marginalized urban youth. Many students develop a sense of their own intelligence based on what their experiences during their school years. Students are generally, even if unconsciously, tracked by teachers and counseling staff. A relatively disproportionate number of African-American and Latino youth are assigned to "lower" classrooms. Whether students are told they are smart and should be preparing to go to college; or whether they are told that they are 'low', students begin to believe what is said about them. In our schools, a student's intelligence is based on factors outside of the student's realm of existence (Hatt, 2007). According to statistics, 40–60 percent of students become "chronically disengaged" by the start of high school (Marks, 2000; Sedlak, 1986). Scholars discuss the lack of intrinsic motivation in students as they leave elementary school and enter the middle school grades (6–8); stating that these years are characterized by a change in motivation and a weakening academic performance (Eccles, 1999; Marks, 2000; Skinner & Belmont, 1993; Wigfield, Eccles, Iver, Reuman & Midgley, 1991). Marks (2000) further expounds that disengagement becomes a "pervasive" problem at the middle school level (p. 156). Thus, due to tracking, our students are losing motivation and are becoming increasingly disengaged with school. The data also reveals that this is occurring at the middle school age level.

Second, in addition to not speaking to the intelligences of our students, we feel that these tests don't represent all aspects of the youth being tested. Granted, Zitlow and Kohn (2000) add that the United States tests students more than any nation in the world. They continue that some of the cause for such testing is likely due to corporate interest, tradition and even the proclivity for Americans to like to attach numbers to things (Zitlow & Kohn, 2000). However, it seems to us that students are multi-faceted and have more talents than just what is represented on the tests. Gardner (2011) agrees, explaining that human beings have multiple intelligences and learn in different ways.

Zitlow and Kohn (2000) also question the objectivity of these tests, the significance of the scores and how serious students take the tests. Some of these thoughts help us to pose questions about how indicative a standardized test is of all youths. Can one method of assessing really give a clear picture of the level of comprehension for every student in a classroom, or a school or even a school district?

Finally, students that may feel marginalized by these traditional forms of assessment can become resentful of the idea of schooling and education in general. In our classrooms, we have observed students unwilling to participate because they feel they will be unsuccessful. Smith (2004) explains that marginalized youth sometimes become "stigmatized and despondent" from current assessment practices (p. 587). Kahl (2013) further explains that the neo-liberal ideas of standardized testing "stifles a critical agenda" and holds students back from actually learning (p. 2613). Eventually, this stifling can lead to students unwillingness to learn, the belief that they are "dumb" and even resentment of school (Hatt, 2007). This cultural bias tends to have the effect of increasing the achievement gap because it causes students to feel less than adequate in spaces of academia, leading to unwanted student outcomes (Hatt, 2007; Walpole et al., 2005).

What's the Science?

So what's the science? The science is applying a pedagogy of youth culture. We believe that when it comes to measuring student achievement, too much emphasis has been placed on data. As a former business analyst, I understand the ease of placing faith in data and numbers. Data is a clean, easy way to make a black and white decision on a singular subject. Placing faith in data is a feasible response in most cases. However, in the case of assessing human beings, we question whether or not data efficiently tells the whole story of a student's assessed skills. As an educator who believes in relationships and care, I must point out that placing faith in data and numbers in the case of student assessment minimizes the importance of the human element. Without the human element as part of this important equation, we negate take into account aspects such as: student health issues, family factors, socio-economic issues, student attitudes, parental involvement, and even funding difficulties. We believe that this is a grave mistake.

In the previous discussion of three characteristics of the current state of assessment, we discussed how assessment today focuses on students all being tested in the same manner. We have been told that this is to ensure fairness among all students. However, in many cases, many students of color or students in urban spaces struggle with these assessments because they cannot relate to the questions. While we agree that some form of assessment is necessary, we believe the method of application should be reformed. Assessment should be commensurate with cultural propensities of students. YCP is characteristic of basing its tenets on relationships. In this case, assessment would be no different. With this in mind, we offer three options for successful assessment practices: First, we must redefine what is considered intelligence. Second, we must revamp assessment practices to cover Gen Z's multiple intelligences. Last, we must omit the cultural bias that is present within current assessment protocols.

Redefine Intelligence

By redefining intelligence, we mean that educational institutions should take into account the multiple intelligences of our students. In the previous section, we discussed the decrease in intrinsic motivation due to some of the tracking systems in the schools. Students sometimes feel that they are "not smart." These feelings can lead to disparagement with school which eventually leads to poor student achievement. Tracking systems that lead students to believe they are "not smart" can often be the cause of some of these feelings.

This tracking system is rooted in the cultural biases of our current educational system. Standardized testing has become a function of this tracking system. It is assumed that students have no cultural value to submit to the educational process. The belief that students have educational value within them has been advanced with Ladson-Billings's (1995) CRP. She illustrates this with a story of a group that she mentored in which members of the group began to assist each other with learning. She was basically a facilitator who guided student growth by letting students use their own stories to cultivate their own learning process. A culturally relevant approach advocates for student learners to share their own story in the classroom. Standardized tests and the current tracking system do not speak to the intelligences of our individualized students.

The idea of changing the definition of what is "smart" based on a student's cultural toolkit could be one such approach. Students from a low-income socio-economic status may not have the same cultural toolkit as a student from an affluent one. However, this does not necessarily mean that one is

better than the other. It just means that they have a different way of prob-
lem-solving and critical thinking. A challenge to the current educational system is for us to find ways to excavate value from both students.

Revamp Assessment by Omitting Cultural Bias

We do not believe that one method of assessing can give a clear picture of
the level of comprehension for every student in a classroom, a school or a
school district. Standardized testing is designed to give an accurate assessment of each student's abilities in a given subject. Scholars have posited that
such testing has long been unable to achieve the desired results (Delpit, 1995;
Hatt, 2007; Kahl, 2013; Kohn, 2000; Walpole et al., 2005). Therefore, as educators of Gen Z students, we should work toward an assessment structure that
encompasses youth culture. Again, John and I do not necessarily believe that
there is one singular assessment practice that will work for every student. On
the contrary, we believe that assessments may need to be as differentiated as
instruction. With this in mind, we believe studying young people's culture
similar to how the marketing and branding companies have done would shed
light on different ways to come up with these differentiated methods.

   While we understand the importance of measuring a student's ability,
our collective approach to measuring these skills must be reformed. Emdin
(2009) has taken such an approach to studying and assessing mathematics
and the sciences. His reality pedagogy builds upon culturally relevant and critical pedagogy, moving beyond efforts to address the challenges within urban
schools that focus on the academic deficiencies of youth to instead support
both teachers and their students in improving their classroom experiences.
His Science Genius program seeks to "meet urban youth who are traditionally disengaged in science classrooms on their cultural turf ..." (Adjapong &
Emdin, 2015, p. 67). Emdin, and his Science Genius team, teaches students
science principles by starting at the students own cultural reference point. He
then assesses by using a cipher to have students either discuss or rhyme about
different concepts in science. He has since taken it to a higher level. Currently, he has a Science Genius B.A.T.T.L.E. This consists of middle and high
school students researching about various scientific principles. The students
then take that research and create rhymes to help facilitate understanding
about those principles. The students then rap those rhymes about science in
front of an audience. By using students cultural capital as a starting point,
they use the students own voice and allow this student to teach what she has

learned in a manner that may be more comfortable than sitting at a desk, taking a traditional test.

According to Delpit (1995) many of these students get a sense of their educational value from what is said about them or how they perceive they are viewed by teachers. In this sense, we advance that a method of assessment that includes aspects of youths lives would facilitate implementation of any testing. This approach would also be a driving force to help omit cultural bias because educators would be basing assessment on student's cultural toolkits. An important first step in an undertaking like this is building those relationships with students.

While we realize that our ideas may seem radical for some, we also realize that the current structure is not achieving results. While the work may be surmountable, if it achieves the sought after results, it will be worth the struggle. Our ideas will need to be fleshed out, however, basing assessment on youth culture has promising undertones. By redefining our overall meaning of intelligence and revamping assessment by omitting cultural biases, we at least take a step in a positive direction.

MC Notes!

"We Ain't Failing" is a song that was directly inspired by my incredible and empowering experience the last five years working as a teaching artist (TA) in the New York City public school system. Over this time I was able to learn a great deal about some of the current challenges in urban public school education in NYC. Through research, I discovered many of the same issues I was dealing with were happening around the globe. The residency this inspiration came directly from is a test preparation program that helps prepare high school students in NYC to pass the statewide standardized Regents Exam in English, U.S. History and global history. The purpose of these sessions is to build connection and community in the classrooms, enhance student engagement, increase student participation and strengthen content knowledge and most of all, BEAT THE TEST (Cherfas, Casciano & Wiggins, 2018). During each residency I would plan at least once a week with my co-teachers and create ways to implement all of these relevant and responsive ideas into lesson plans that also aligned with the common core standards and delivered academic rigor with a non-traditional approach. What follows are a few of the observations which I made during this time.

Building Community in the Classroom

A simple method that usually works well for me is to always give the class-room teacher a role in the class, especially in the activities. For example imagine the very straight forward traditional teacher freestyle rapping in class about the content or acting out a historic figure or character in a book in a fun theatrical manner. This will not only bring more creative edge to the teachers overall delivery but it will also allow the students to see their teacher in a different and "cooler" scenario. Anytime students see teachers genuinely interested in what they care about aka youth culture, it builds a connection that can potentially be the entry point to the most powerful ways to reach ones students.

During all of my residencies, I have spoken with many students about the challenges of the Regents Exam. So far students have expressed issues of poor teacher-student relationships, delivery of the content, disliking the teacher, not being interested in the material because it wasn't engaging or didn't relate to them in any way. The students couldn't see themselves in the work so therefore deemed it unimportant and useless. When I first began this journey, the major reality check for me was that most of the students I was working with were students who had already taken and failed this exam up to three or more times. Therefore, many of the students were already mentally defeated and believed they weren't intelligent enough to ever pass this exam. This reality was a major concern for me as I began to realize that I was there to deliver much more than what I was expecting to share. A lot of my classes were spent encouraging the students in general to get them re-motivated to believe again that with hard work and consistency that they could beat the test. I would tell all the students that beating the test literally started with their mindset of the exam. I let them know how important it was to begin by telling them to say to themselves out loud that they believed they could do it. Without that simple belief, passing the exam was nearly impossible.

Next, I realized that once students were introduced to the information in a manner that was familiar to them, they began to gain interest in topics that otherwise didn't engage them. My goal was to allow these students who had a mostly negative experience in their school careers to celebrate learning successfully. Moreover, if a student gets an incorrect answer in class, I work to ensure that I do not embarrass them and discourage them from future partici-pation. Instead I would encourage them to think more critically to get to the right answer or at least closer to understanding the material.

Use What They Know

One of the things I tell students who are literally stuck in High School due to not passing the Regents Exam, is to view this as one of the many obstacles that they as young adults have faced outside of school. Also respect the process and the discipline it takes to be consistent enough to beat the test or any obstacle for the most part. It is disheartening to observe students, who for so long have been told that they are not intelligent, begin to embrace and carry around these falsehoods about themselves. I never look at any student who walks into a classroom as an empty vessel that has no prior knowledge what so ever and therefore can't learn.

I feel that most of the foundational academics that urban students need for school, they already have. However, they usually don't understand how to connect and translate this information. For example many students are said to not know geography from a traditional stand point. However these same students easily understand that Kendrick Lamar is from Compton which is in Southern California right outside of Los Angeles, on the West Coast near the Pacific Ocean. Or that Drake is from Toronto which is in Canada, which is within North America and is located north of New York City. Another example is how many students can better identify with percentages when viewed from a sports or even a retail perspective. For example, if Stephan Curry of the Golden State Warriors made 7 out of 10 three point attempts, what percentage did he shoot in the game? The list of possible examples such as this goes on and on.

I also made a few more observations. Once in the classrooms working with the teacher and the students, I discovered that the best academic resources available for teachers to use to prepare their students for the exams were usually not available due to lack of funds or just negligence overall. This made me wonder how many urban schools face this same issue which is basically causing our students to attempt these exams feeling unprepared because the materials they are learning and studying from are outdated or don't speak to the Exam productively. However schools that are in more affluent areas don't face these problems at all.

Another thing I noticed, many of the so-called "failing" students that I met over the years were already great researchers. They just researched in a non-traditional sense. All of them are strapped with lots of information surrounding any subject that directly interest them. If they didn't have the info already, they all knew how to get it very quickly. These students are extremely technologically savvy and they know it. I still hear many stories from students talking about how they would have to set up their parents tech devices because their parents were clueless with how to set up and or use any of the devices their own. The moment that I began to help students better understand how their prior knowledge and experiences translate in school is when I began to witness the real magic of this journey. When the students were able to create around any of the content we are studying in class they were able to internalize the experience and truly learn it for themselves. Before, students were just learning the material enough to spit it back out on a test and never remember it or use it ever again. These creative classes taught me that whether the students were writing poems, songs or raps or they were creating and acting out theatrical skits, they were able to engage with the material and connect to it in a way that they were unable to before.

Use a Hook to Tie into the Lesson

A direct example of this experience would be teaching a subject like World Wars in History. I would use Rap, Reality Show and/or Social Media Beefs as a hook into the lesson. By the time the students start to share their thoughts on these topics that they're usually all very well versed in, they began to bring up a lot of the major concepts that relate to World Wars. So now they are able to think critically around concepts like territories (turf wars), allies (crew, entourage), nationalism (Pride), causes leading up to the conflict and much more. Most of the time when I started the class with a hook that the students were familiar with already and then I connect it to the content that relates to the class/exam, it was a lot easier for students to remember and understand the concepts better. Connecting these academic concepts that before seemed very unfamiliar and complex to information that the students had prior to entering the classroom now allows them to connect with this material like they never thought was possible.

Audi 5000

We know you ain't failin'! Now we got to make sure our students ain't failin'. How do we do that? It begins with redefining intelligence within our schools. Many students in urban spaces come to school with street sense. For instance, these students may not know all about world history and understand the concept of Allies and Axis, but they can tell you all about reality TV and hip-hop beefs. We can use these parallels to help them understand the concept of Allies and Axis powers by using their prior knowledge. To help internalize the material, we can take these concepts and create materials which touch upon multiple intelligences such as a rhyme, skit, etc. Once students actually use what they know to facilitate learning the material, they never forget it. It becomes a part of their lives.

Dr. Emdin said that "We Ain't Failing" is an affirmation! It's a battle cry for our students and for teachers who refuse to allow the system to fail our students. It's our way of redefining the idea of intelligence when it comes to urban students. When we redefine intelligence to fit what these students already know, we give them an equal chance to be successful. Assessments that relate to students cultural tendencies are not only fair but they are over-due. A couple of questions remain, (1) is it easier to keep our assessments as is because it makes it easier for us to create and manage? (2) Does big business tend to lose money if we switch up our assessment approach? We can all spec-ulate the answers. But one thing remains true, it really depends on us. Are we in it for ourselves or for our students?

Interlude 3: No Phones, No Headphones, No Future

No Phones, No Headphones No Future is a song that was directly inspired by my experience over the last five plus years. Working as a teaching artist in middle school or high school in New York City, I constantly see signs instruct-ing students to put away their technology. These signs basically tell students that the technology side of their lives, with which they are most familiar, is not welcome in school. Items such as headphones, phones or tablets, anything tech based was not allowed in school. This makes technology seem as if it was something that was dumbed down or not welcome or even a distraction in school. In every school I walked into, I would just see similar posters or signs on the walls. They would have a picture of anything that students engage with on a daily basis with a red circle and a cross through it. What bothered me most about seeing these signs posted is the idea that this could hinder the growth and development of young people getting into or learning more about technology and communication. Students need knowledge of these devices to be relevant in society, later in life and to be savvy with the times. We are in a time in which all of these gadgets and social media marketing tools are being used by the top companies in the world to market, connect and communicate with people. A lot of our young people are technologically genius with this material and just understand this. To steer them away from this is not smart. Especially if we understand that many of the jobs these young people will have don't even exist yet. That's how fast technology is moving.

Technology isn't necessarily innovation. You can't just bring these different iPads and phones or different means of engaging with young people with technology into the classroom and think that that's being innovative. You must actually have the protocol and designed implementation to activate these things and make them productive and useful. I noticed that usually in school today when any cyberbullying programs or presentations around technology is ever delivered in school, it's always coming from the perspective of the negative aspects of using social media and the internet. The focus is usually on all of the non-productive things that you can do in that realm rather than giving them actually the powerful productive ways that you can use this as a tool in a resource to empower your regular life and your school life. Using technology to teach students to be able to be more efficient and technologically savvy is not done enough. We are teaching 21st century students with 20th century resources. I always say that we're delivering Flintstones era to our students who are living in The Jetsons times. We're literally giving them this prehistoric or traditional way that's been developed hundreds of years ago versus actually innovating our practices and being able to engage them in the ways that they're more familiar with. I feel like this is a disservice to a lot of our students. Many times technology is looked at as the one and only answer. I don't believe that it's the one and only answer but it is a great entry point and it's a way to actually allow young people to engage in school and probably perform better.

For instance, during multiple choice tests, I've use clickers or apps like Zaption and Blippar. There are many different types of apps that use augmented reality or virtual reality. These apps can allow us to innovate the assessment situation. Let's take it away from just a number 2 pencil or a scantron sheet and actually take it to a level where we're innovating how we even give students tests or exams. Sometimes, I've even turned a review before the Regents exam into a game show. This allowed me to focus on different parts of the exam such as multiple choice, short answer response or even outlining of an essay. I would use prompts that would be on the exam, but given in a game show format to just make it fun and deliver it in a different way. But the bottom line is, technology is ruling the world and we can't escape it and I feel like it's time for the system to catch up. Technology is moving so fast that if the educational system stays on this path, we will not be able to catch up to where our students are today. And when we do catch up, the students will be somewhere else. We really have to think about these things wisely. I say no phones, no headphones, no future because many educators and many leaders in the Department of Education are ignoring the need to update and innovate. We need to change the fact that some students feel unwelcomed in unsafe and unwanted in these learning spaces.

References

Adjapong, E., & Emdin, C. (2015). Rethinking pedagogy in urban spaces: implementing hip-hop pedagogy in the urban science classroom. *Journal of Urban Learning Teaching and Research, 11*, 66–77.

Cherfas, L., Casciano, R., & Wiggins, M. A. (2018). It's bigger than hip-hop: Estimating the impact of a culturally responsive classroom intervention on student outcomes. *Urban Education*, 1–34.

Delpit, L. D. (1995). *Other people's children: Cultural conflict in the classroom*. New York, NY: New Press.

Eccles, J. S. (1999). The development of children ages 6 to 14. *The Future of Children When School Is Out, 9*(2), 30–44.

Emdin, C. (2009). Rethinking student participation: A model from hip-hop and urban science education. *Edge Phi Delta Kappa International, 5*(1), 1–18.

Gardner, H. (2011). *Frames of mind: The theory of multiple intelligences*. New York, NY: Basic Books.

Hatt, B. (2007). Street smarts vs. book smarts: The figured world of smartness in the lives of marginalized, urban youth. *The Urban Review, 39*(2), 145–166.

Kahl, D. (2013). Critical communication pedagogy and assessment: Reconciling two incongruous ideas. *International Journal of Communication, 7*, 2610–2630.

Ladson-Billings, G. (1995). Toward a theory of culturally relevant pedagogy. *American Educational Research Journal, 32*(3), 465–491.

Marks, H. M. (2000). Student engagement in instructional activity: Patterns in the elementary, middle, and high school years. *American Educational Research Journal, 37*(1), 153–184.

Sedlak, M. W. (1986). *Selling students short: Classroom bargains and academic reform in the American high school*. New York, NY: Teachers College Press.

Skinner, E. A., & Belmont, M. J. (1993). Motivation in the classroom: Reciprocal effects of teacher behavior and student engagement across the school year. *Journal of educational psychology, 85*(4), 571.

Smith, M. K. (2004). Nel Noddings, the ethics of care and education. *The Encyclopedia of Informal Education*.

Walker, T. (2016, March 09). Survey: 70 percent of educators say state assessments not developmentally appropriate. Retrieved from http://neatoday.org/2016/02/18/standardized-tests-not-developmentally-appropriate/

Walpole, M., Mcdonough, P. M., Bauer, C. J., Gibson, C., Kanyi, K., & Toliver, R. (2005). This test is unfair. *Urban Education*, 40(3), 321–349.

Wigfield, A., Eccles, J. S., Mac Iver, D., Reuman, D. A., & Midgley, C. (1991). Transitions during early adolescence: Changes in children's domain-specific self perceptions and general self-esteem across the transition to junior highschool. *Developmental Psychology*, 27(4), 552.

Winner, E. (1997). Exceptionally high intelligence and schooling. *American Psychologist*, 52(10), 1070–1081.

Zitlow, C. S., & Kohn, A. (2001). The case against standardized testing: Raising the scores, ruining the schools. *The English Journal*, 91(1), 112.

· 6 ·

B PLAN

"You never once considered that probably the lesson wouldn't resonate in class so vibrantly, that's why u gotta keep a variety of lessons and activities vitally, or get caught looking real indecisive B ..."

Say What?

Over the past several chapters, we have discussed our thoughts on relating to and understanding our 21st century students. As previously discussed, the topics in these chapters are generated from our personal experiences as educators. This chapter continues to build from our experiences. We offer an analysis on the process of class preparation for an educator who chooses to enact the tenets of YCP.

As a teacher, we acknowledge that it can be easy to get into a rut when you teach a group of students each day. In his rhymes on the song "Don't Smile Till November," John expressed that teaching is a love sport. However, even if you love teaching; when you have to organize, create structure and routines for a group of young people (or any people for that matter); it's easy to focus on just the organization, structures and routines. The goal is to ensure that students receive instruction daily and that we as teacher's are following state guidelines for curriculum. During our discussion, we were able to step back and take a look at ourselves in addition to what we observed in our schools. Some of our observations included teachers and administrators with monotonous routines, making assumptions about what young people relate to and offering limited student voice/expression.

Part of our research for this book included reflecting on items and events we noticed in our schools. One of the issues that John and I discussed was our observations of teachers in the classroom. We discussed everything from everyday struggles of teachers in the classroom to struggles with balancing instruction and administrative policies. In our conversations, we also discussed the significance of planning in relation to a smooth classroom. We compared and contrasted days we considered to be successful and unsuccessful in our classroom. We noticed days that went well usually occurred when we were well prepared. Moreover, we found that we also had better days in the classroom when we focused on *how* we delivered our plan. We thought; let's discuss in depth what worked for us in our classrooms. Particularly, we were interested in figuring out how we implemented our plans with success.

While there are many facets to class preparation, we will primarily discuss lesson planning. However, this chapter will not focus on the traditional "how to" of lesson planning. There are many books that can provide insight on creating lesson plans. Rather we will touch on lesson plan implementation and dive into the process with which one implements lesson plans (or what we call, lesson delivery). We will particularly zero in on the reality of actually being in the classroom and how one's original plan can get sidetracked or simply not work (Farrell, 2002). We will discuss reasons to change a lesson plan and give suggestions on ideas for having a back-up plan (B Plan) when ones planned lesson does not work. Lastly, we will discuss controllable items during a lesson that a teacher can control to help make the lesson run more smoothly. We will frame these items within the tenets for YCP.

What's the Deal?

Classroom lesson planning generally involves listing objectives for a certain program (Farrell, 2002). Farrell (2002) defines a daily lesson plan as "a written description of how students will move toward attaining specific objectives" (p. 30). Most lesson plans are written in terms of daily, weekly or quarterly. Some teachers may plan their lessons by a learning unit while others may base them on a specific theme (Farrell, 2002; Yinger, 1978). As previously mentioned, we will not focus on these mechanics of lesson planning. Instead, we will discuss the process of lesson plan implementation and why considering youth culture in the implementation process is beneficial to both the student and the teacher.

Lesson Plan Implementation and Delivery

Going back to the mid-20th century, scholars have theorized on the importance of teacher thought processes in the classroom (Clark & Yinger, 1979; Clark & Peterson, 1986). In a landmark 1968 study, the importance of the teacher's thinking processes on classroom processes came to light (Clark & Peterson, 1986; Jackson, 2009). With this understanding, these thought processes were determined to be made up of three distinct components. First, teacher planning (preactive and interactive) is an integral part of their process. Second, teacher's innermost thoughts and ideas affect their process. Lastly, their processes are affected tremendously by their beliefs, values and culture (Clark & Peterson, 1986).

Clark and Peterson (1986) describe the preactive planning as preparation done before class. They further describe interactive planning as adjustments made while working with students (Clark & Peterson, 1986). This distinction, discussed over thirty years prior to this manuscript, is important because it identifies a difference between planning and making on the spot adjustments. When John says in the song *B Plan*, "you never once considered that probably, the lesson wouldn't have resonated in class so vibrantly." we are acknowledging that more often than not, teachers need to make adjustments to their plans. Currently, pre-service teachers are taught how to create lesson plans (the preactive portion). However, we suggest that pre-service teachers should be given guidelines about working toward the interactive portion of a lesson. In addition to teaching pre-service teachers to create a lesson plan, shouldn't we also be teaching them how to improve their process of lesson plan implementation?

While it goes without saying that a teachers innermost thoughts affect their processes; the effect of beliefs, values and cultures on classrooms has been studied numerous times. The thoughts of a teacher including their biases, fears and predications all come into play as they plan lessons. In order to navigate these biases etc., teachers rely on their beliefs, values and cultural sensibilities. Thus, beliefs, values and culture closely tie into these innermost thoughts. Richards, Gallo and Renandya (2001) explain that teacher beliefs play a pivotal role in their practices and that personal and professional factors impact planning and processes.

We suggest arming pre-service teachers with ideas and activities designed to assist them while they are actually teaching using the lesson plan. Since most lessons do not go according to plan, teachers need to be prepared to perform on the fly. As performing artists, we found this to be the case on many occasions. With a primary focus on lesson plan implementation, we believe that the aforementioned ideas about teacher processes directly affect our conversation on using youth culture in lesson planning. More specifically, it speaks to the importance of teacher beliefs within education. We believe it is imperative for successful teachers to value youth culture. To try to implement YCP and not have a belief in the importance of youth culture may be a difficult task. The next section will include a discussion of how YCP can be intertwined with implementation processes, reasons to change a lesson plan during class.

Reasons to Adjust the Lesson Plan

This section will include a discussion of how YCP can be intertwined with implementation processes, reasons to change a lesson plan during class. The delivery of the lesson plan is probably one of the most important aspects of teaching besides creating the actual plan. During our observations, we noticed that when a teacher delivers the plan with enthusiasm and excitement, students are normally engaged. The same holds true when a teacher implements her plan with a lack of enthusiasm.

Lesson plan delivery involves a structured process in which the teacher intently delivers the plan in a certain way. Eye contact, tone of voice and movement all play a crucial role in the delivery of one's lesson plan (Snow & Campbell, 2017). Writers have compared teachers to actors performing on a stage (Cavanagh, 2017; Delisio, 2007). Teachers about to deliver a new lesson may have the same apprehensions and even fears as an actor about to hit the stage. Cavanagh (2017) asserts that "teaching is acting" (p. 1). She goes on to explain that teaching is like acting because both tap "into your true emotions and [connect] with your audience on an authentic level" (p. 1). Since both John and I are performers, we bring that element of our stage performance to our pedagogy.

On stage, we perform for our audience. With that in mind, we view our students as our audience. We bring our hip-hop stage performance to the classroom to help deliver our lesson plan. This is how we use hip-hop in our classroom. We perform for our students to keep them engaged and involved in order to make a connection with them. However, as with some shows, sometimes, that connection is a bit harder to make. As with one of our performances, if we don't have the audience engaged, then we have to change our show or change our approach to that particular show. This is no different than being in the classroom. If the lesson is not working, then that teacher must change the show.

Farrell (2002) asserts "when a lesson is not succeeding, teachers should make immediate adjustments to the original plan" (p. 34). While there can be many reasons to make a change in a lesson plan in the middle of giving the lesson, we will speak on three main reasons. First, the lesson is obviously going badly. Second, something may have happened in the class or at the start of class that necessitates improvisation. And lastly, there may be a current event that relates to your students and needs to be addressed right away. This could be something that occurs in the community or even a big global event. As a teacher, or even as a performer, you know when you are losing your audience. As with either, when you are noticing several side conversations or looks of bewilderment, you inherently know that something is going awry. It is at this point that you must have a B Plan. You need some other way to recapture your audience's attention.

Usually during a lesson one can tell if it is obviously going badly. This is easy to notice because you will have lost the attention of most of your students or the majority of the class does not understand your concept. Implementation of a B Plan in an instance such as this could be as simple as restarting the lesson or stopping the lesson and asking students to explain what parts of the lesson they understand. Then the teacher can use that as the new starting point. We will go through some ideas in the next section.

When an unusual event happens during class or at the start of class, that event may sometime dictate that the teacher change up the lesson plan. This could be as simple as something abnormal occurring during the course of the school day. Sometimes these things could be a fight, a rumor that is going around the school or it could be something positive that has all the students' attention at the moment. Sometimes, it is difficult to regain focus when an event such as these occurs. It may be best to "go with the flow" and have a class discussion on that event. This aligns with YCP because such a class discussion may help the teacher get a better understanding of her students and possibly allow the teacher to demonstrate her level of care. It also increases potential to build relationships. Additionally, every once in a while, a major current world or global event that relates to your students may need to be addressed right away. This could even be something that occurs in the community. These types of events may be tragic or so joyful that students are excited to speak about them. These are great opportunities to turn into teachable moments.

Controllable Items

Notwithstanding, the best preparation and delivery methods work much more fluidly if you consider controllable items to help make the class run smoothly ahead of time. The lesson plan is a map and can help a teacher think about content, materials, sequencing and timing (Farrell, 2002). Farrell (2002) states that lesson variety and pace are two important factors to consider when delivering lesson plans. One's goal with a lesson is to deliver an activity that will keep the class lively and interesting. YCP with its focus on youth culture, relationships and care align with controlling pace and lesson variety. In the next section, we further tie these concepts to YCP.

What's the Science?

So what's the science? The science is applying pedagogy of youth culture. YCP can add a multi-faceted element to lesson plan implementation and delivery. With its focus on relationships and care, YCP is the perfect complement to lesson plan delivery and implementation because it fosters a student-centered approach to education. YCP embraces adjustments to lesson plan change because YCP says the teacher is on stage. When emcees are on stage, sometimes they freestyle, or make up a rhyme off the top of their head without writing it down on paper. Sometimes, they have to change a song or change the flow of the show in order to keep the audience engaged. It's a hip-hop "thing" to be able to "freestyle." This is comparable to a teacher making an adjustment to a lesson plan in progress. Sometimes, teachers must change the flow in order to keep their audience engaged.

With respects to lesson plan creation, YCP dictates that educators make preactive lesson plans based around youth culture. Creating lesson plans in this manner allows the teacher to make a plan that may already inherently hold student interest. While students may not be interested in the subject matter, the lesson may still hold their interest because of the way the information is delivered. For instance, let's use our previous example of understanding world wars. When John teaches a lesson on World Wars, he would parallel it with a rap/social media beef. This is an example of using hip-hop aesthetics and culture to deliver a lesson. Whether these lessons include a game or an activity, create the lesson in a way that will hold student interest.

Conversely, during the time in which students are not in tune with the current lesson (and these times will occur), Clark and Peterson's (1986) description of interactive lesson planning aligns with YCP's premise of performing on stage. A teacher should make the adjustment immediately if she notices that she is losing her audience, just like an emcee. When a teacher does adjust the lesson plan, YCP framework may call for an activity based on something going on in youth culture at the time. There may be a point at which you change the activity to one that may better align with youth culture. For instance, choose an activity based on something that is a current trend or style such as fidget spinners or the water bottle challenge.

Moreover, a method of YCP also calls for educators to mix it up! There is a diverse group of learners in your classroom, make sure you are touching the different areas of learning in your lesson implementation and delivery. A teacher should be actively working to touch upon Gardner's (2011) multiple intelligences (Verbal/Linguistic, Bodily/Kinesthetic, Visual/Spatial, Musical/Rhythmic, Logical/Mathematical, Interpersonal, Intrapersonal and Naturalistic) at some point in every lesson. As each student undoubtedly learns by several of these modes of learning, this ensures that the teacher is uses them all at some point.

To sum things up, earlier in the book, we talked about making the student the center of one's classroom pedagogy. This certainly applies to lesson implementation and delivery. Often times, teachers bring in materials they assume will be relatable to their students, instead of asking the students what interests them. Many times a classroom discussion or a quick listen to classroom chatter can give teachers clues as to what may hold student interest in classwork. Moreover, in conjunction with letting one's students be at the forefront of the classroom, get students involved. Young people are connected and can have successful communication with each other. Try letting them explain concepts and ideas to each other whether in groups or teaching the class. This enables your students to feel like they are a part of the classroom and ties in most of what we have been discussing on YCP. Adjustments to your lesson or a "B Plan" are essential to any good pedagogical process. There are many unforeseeable factors that can call for a need to adjust one's plan. Being open minded to adjustments and allowing one's students to be the focal point of that adjustment are the premise of YCP.

MC Notes!

"When you're on your way to school and everything's in a flow but you realize you left todays lesson plan home, you need a B Plan, a B Plan"

"When you got class in session and everything is alright, but your students fell asleep cause they're not feeling the vibes, you need a B Plan, a B Plan"

The original idea for the B Plan concept came directly from a conversation that J Rawls, Sadat X (Brand Nubian) and I were having while in Columbus, Ohio for a show a couple of summers ago. Sadat, who is also an educator, was speaking about his experience in class on a lesson he thought would resonate with the students, but things don't actually go according to plan. During this rundown of his school day he yells out "You gotta have a B Plan because sometimes, the kids just don't feel it." As soon as he said that about having a B Plan, Rawls and I looked at each other and knew immediately that this was a concept that we would revisit for the YCP project. B Plan is also inspired by my personal experience during my early teaching practices.

During my humble beginnings of teaching I've had several classes in which I assumed that what I had planned would work well with the students. Sometimes it worked and other times it didn't work. After going through several scenarios of my lesson not resonating with the class, it taught me that I needed to have more options on deck. Whether it was delivering the lesson in a different way, having a completely different lesson or having an arsenal of activities, I wanted to be sure that I was always connecting to Youth Culture and what was familiar to the students. All I knew is that I didn't like that feeling of looking unprepared to the students. Once they realized that I wasn't sure of what to do next then it was very difficult to keep their attention.

A great analogy for the B Plan concept is as follows: If you were a quarterback in the NFL and you called a play (plan) but you noticed the defense is on to your next move; you would then call an audible which allows your team to know to switch it up, increasing the chances of making a great play. This works similar in the classroom. If you clearly see that your plan is not working, don't force it. Instead be overly prepared with options. Once I gained more experience and became more confident in my teaching abilities, I began to use activities that were fun, interactive and connected to the concepts that we are learning. This became my go to. I would also pay lots of attention to what worked and what didn't work well with my students.

My efforts to be overly prepared were inspired by the Trayvon Martin and Mike Brown cases in which both boys were shot and killed by law enforcement. I can remember coming into class during these specific incidents and hearing the chatter throughout the room; which included everything from concern to being emotional and wanting to talk about these matters. I then realized that school doesn't often consider creating a safe space where students can unpack many of the societal ills that they witness and are exposed to regularly. When the above-mentioned scenarios occurred, I knew that I couldn't just ignore the reality these young people were dealing with. It was apparent that I had to change the lesson and allow my students to express their feelings about these incidents. The harsh reality of this perspective is that although I used these specific tragic situations, there have been countless examples that fit perfectly into this same situation and the list goes on.

Young people in the communities directly affected by this type of violence are expected to excel in their academics without ever considering their mental health and overall well-being. This is the very sentiment that inspires me to have a solid, empathetic approach to teaching and interacting in the urban school settings, which I am involved. I began to do this by telling the students that I am them, because I am. Just like them I was their age in the public school system in New York City dealing with a lot of the same pressures in and out of school. As our classroom communities have become stronger, I was able to make it a regular thing to have a social justice layer of activities and instruction in every lesson plan. This allowed my teaching style to embody a safe space for my students to express themselves and unpack. I feel needs to exist much more in schools across the world. Youth today, globally, are exposed to much more than we can imagine just based on technologically alone.

So essentially, the message of B Plan is to not only be prepared with various lesson plans and approaches to deliver content, but also build an arsenal of youth culture based activities that resonate with your students. During the process of building this arsenal, pay attention to what works and what doesn't and revisit the material that works using elements of that to create other activities as well. Another thing to consider, survey your students for ideas based on their interest. This can save valuable class time as well. Lastly, I want to add the importance of teachers and administrators being mindful and selfless enough to open your hearts and mind to fully understand the need to create a space for students to unpack issues relating to violence, social justice and many other realities students face every day.

Audi 5000

We want you to have a B Plan! Let's face it, our students are smart and can recognize when we aren't prepared. Having your B Plan ready is better for you and better for your students. It gives you the chance to eliminate insecurity and instability within your class. Moreover, the B Plan is a terrific way to try different things in your classroom and incorporate youth culture into your class. We truly believe that the best lesson plans allow for flexibility and the ability to be flexible really starts with the teacher. Are you in it for yourself or for your students? If you are reading this book, we are willing to bet you are in it for your students.

References

Cavanagh, S. (2017, June 27). All the Classroom's a Stage. Retrieved from https://www.chronicle.com/article/All-the-Classroom-s-a-Stage/240429

Clark, C. M., & Peterson, P. L. (1986). Teachers' thought processes. In M. C. Wittrock (Ed.), *Handbook of research on teaching (3rd ed.)*. New York, NY: Macmillan.

Clark, C., & Yinger, R. (1979) *Three studies of teachers planning, research series 55*. East Lansing, MI: Michigan State University.

Delisio, E. (2007, May 9). Using acting skills in the classroom. Retrieved from https://www.educationworld.com/a_issues/chat/chat213.shtml

Farrell, T. (2002). Lesson planning. In J. C. Richards & W. A Renandya (Eds), *Methodology in language teaching: An anthology of current practice* (pp. 30–39). New York, NY: Cambridge University Press.

Gardner, H. (2011). *Frames of mind: The theory of multiple intelligences*. New York, NY: Basic Books.

Jackson, P. W. (2009). *Life in classrooms: Reissued with a new introduction*. New York, NY: Teachers College Press.

Richards, J. C., Gallo, P. B., & Renandya, W. A. (2001). Exploring teachers' beliefs and the processes of change. *PAC Journal, 1*(1), 41–58.

Snow, D. B., & Campbell, M. (2017). *More than a native speaker: An introduction to teaching English abroad*. Alexandria, VA: Tesol Press.

Yinger, R. J. (1978). *A study of teacher planning: Description and model of preactive decision making*. East Lansing, MI: Institute for Research on Teaching, Michigan State University.

· 7 ·

GET ON BOARD

"See nowadays we don't have too many choices, invest in the future and help the youth discover their voices, defining their alternative identities and live joyous, we came to tell you about YCP and its importance."

Say What?

With the ongoing struggles of teaching in urban classrooms today, teachers need all the support they can get to be successful. In professional development classes, teachers are constantly taught "best practices" in the areas of classroom management, behavior management, instruction, etc. However, one aspect of teaching we believe gets overlooked the most is the human element. Teachers and students are human. Human beings thrive off relationships, care and social interaction (Noddings, 2005). If these concepts are forgotten then teaching can fall into a behavioristic framework that can become stagnant, unforgiving and at times, hostile. We aim to push using a relational framework of teaching that is fluid and allows both teachers and students to learn from one another. For too long interactions in schools have been one-sided in which the approach is for only the teacher to give knowledge or information to the student. As part of reality pedagogy, Emdin speaks on using a transactional approach to teaching in which both the teacher and the student gain something from their interaction (Elon University, 2012).

We believe that this approach takes into account the human element that is often forgotten. But for you to fully understand and grasp the premise of this book, we feel it important to take a step back and give you a little more background on ourselves. We do this to give you more insight into how we formed our philosophies and also to give you more incentive to give our methods a try in your classroom or with your children.

J Rawls

John and I have been teaching for a combined 20 years. However, we both did not begin our careers in education. I completed my business degree from the University of Cincinnati in 1997. Upon graduation, I had every intention of becoming a successful computer programmer/businessman. However, once I entered that industry, I was unfulfilled. I did not enjoy my job and never felt a sense of purpose going to work each day. My cousin suggested that I should try teaching. I never thought about being a teacher but was so unhappy that I decided to give it a try. I instantly fell in love. This was the job for me. The relationship building, the social interaction and the lives that I could change (the human element) made all the difference in the world for me. I finally felt a sense of purpose going to work every day. During all this time, I was blessed to be able to create music. As a producer and DJ, I worked with several hip-hop and soul acts. This eventually gave me an opportunity to travel the world. So since 1998, I have been professionally releasing music as J Rawls; and in 2002, I began my teaching career.

I started out in a small charter school in Columbus, Ohio. I taught 4th and 5th grade for 4 years until they realized that I had a computer background. After that, they tapped me to assist as the Information Technology person as well. I was no longer in the classroom, but I still worked with teachers to ensure the technology in their rooms was working correctly. During this time, I also served in an administrative capacity for the school. I learned so much valuable information as to how schools run and how funding and financing in schools works. After completing my master's degree, I began working for a major district in central Ohio. It was during these experiences that I really began to sink my teeth into teaching all grades. I taught middle and high school business and at the same time, started as an adjunct teacher for college. Keep in mind that all during this time, I am working as a hip-hop and soul producer. I began to produce for acts such as Diamond D, Sadat X, Beastie Boys, El Da Sensei, Eric Roberson, Aloe Blacc, John Robinson, Wordsworth, Masta Ace and more. I also begin to tour with my group Lone Catalysts and as a DJ, I travelled to Europe, Japan, Brazil and even Iceland; all in the name of hip-hop.

Around 2010, Twitter was becoming more popular. I found a chat on Twitter because I followed Sam Seidel, who had written an incredible book about remixing how we think about education at the high school level (Seidel, 2011). It was through Sam that I discovered the weekly #HipHopEd chat group. I began following and sometimes participating in this group and began to learn some of the work of the people involved, like Emery Petchauer, Bettina Love, Martha Diaz and Chris Emdin. I eventually drummed up enough courage to reach out to both of Emery, Chris and Sam on Twitter just to tell them that I admired their work. To my surprise, all three of them were familiar with my work in hip-hop! This really hit home when I met Petchauer and Emdin at The Hip-Hop Literacies Conference at The Ohio State University later that year. This is really the first time that I remember both my academia and hip-hop worlds crossing paths.

By the time I read most of the work of these guys and others, I had decided that I wanted to pursue my doctorate in education. I was inspired. I wanted to add to the academy in the same way that I was driven to add to hip-hop. Since then, these two activities have been fueling my existence. Since completing my Master of Education degree in 2006, I have longed to combine my two passions, hip-hop and education. My journey both led me to many A-alikes in the industry. But John and I noticed that we had many similar journeys throughout hip-hop and eventually, education.

John Robinson

My educator journey officially began in 2011 working as a Teaching Artist (TA) with a small Brooklyn, New York based performing arts organization. The program operated three times a week during after school hours. The initiative was to introduce or develop students in music production, recording, performance, film, photography and more. Each semester the goal was to create an all student music and documentary project. At the end of the residency we would celebrate with a showcase for all the students to show their work to an audience of parents, family, friends, educator staff and the community. In 2012 a colleague introduced me to another amazing opportunity that went much deeper into academia. As previously mentioned, this residency was a test preparation program for the statewide standardized regent's exam in English, U.S. and global history that was designed for New York City high school students at risk of ageing out of school. The program was designed to have a TA teamed up with a Department of Education certified co-teacher and collaborate on both planning and teaching. While leaning on them as the content expert, I was responsible for working with my co-teacher to plan and to innovate the classroom experience using various cultural sensibilities and technologies that are directly aligned with both hip-hop and youth culture. This was all done while catering to the various learning styles that were present in these classrooms. I brought in music for the auditory learners, videos and images for the visual learners and get up out of your seat activities for the kinesthetic learners.

This journey is still one of passion, humility and learning and has led me to being a guest panelist at 2015 SXSW EDU. The panel, titled "Can Hip Hop Save Us? Youth & School Culture" discussed hip-hop's ability to better connect educators and students as well as help prepare students for life, college and careers. I have also been able to share a lot of the methodology I've learned over the past several years via professional development workshops with both parents and teachers. I truly understand that teaching is a love sport and I must thank so many powerful and amazing educators that inspire me every day from their work and the foundation that has been laid. I am very grateful to be connected to this movement of innovative and Hip-Hop Based Education and I look forward to continuing to empower myself as an educator and share with others around the world. Although I have learned a lot over the past five years from hands on experience in many classrooms all over New York City, I understand that there is so much more to learn and I am thankful to have been under the study of mentors like James Miles aka The Fresh Professor, Chennits Pettigrew (Chen Lo), Eboni Hogan and many others. From these HHBE Super Heroes I gained much insight that helped me grow a foundation as an educator and set me on this amazing journey.

JayARE

While we don't claim to have the end-all-be-all approach to teaching, we both have a passion for education. We both also have a passion for hip-hop and we combine them to reach urban youth on a daily basis in schools in Brooklyn, New York and Columbus, Ohio. With that being said, we would like to introduce you to our philosophy of education. We call our philosophy Youth Culture Pedagogy, or YCP for short. From our experiences, we believe the mechanics of teaching are not where the problem lies; it appears to be the methods. Behaviorist frameworks do not make allowances for the human element. We believe that YCP can be the bridge to Generation Z and beyond because it gives the educator a way to stay in tune with the youth that they are teaching. It allows the teacher to use students' prior knowledge, build relationships and express care to all students. We aim to keep that human element at the forefront of our thinking. This chapter is intended give you a brief glimpse into why we think you should get on board with the YCP approach to education that we have outlined in this book.

What's the Deal?

Again, we are not claiming to invent the wheel on youth culture and HHBE. But the purpose of this book is to present a fresh take on why educators should not discount the culture of youth within the classroom. Since many of the youth in marginalized schools identify with hip-hop culture, we feel the use of hip-hop as a tool in education could be a valuable asset. We want to speak to current, future and contemplating teachers and administrators; as well as parents. While we want to reach students with our work, we feel it is imperative to ensure that educators understand the importance of this culturally relevant pedagogy. It is our intent that educators use our ideas and principles to help guide their instruction to further enhance the education process of marginalized urban youth.

What's the Science?

So what's the science? The science is applying a pedagogy of youth culture. As previously stated, this book attempts to root the foundation of youth culture pedagogy within the context of reality pedagogy (Emdin, 2016), culturally responsive pedagogy (Ladson-Billings, 1995b), and HHBE (Hill, 2009; Petchauer, 2009; Hill & Petchauer, 2015). We also aim to align the motivation behind our ideas within relational pedagogy and care ethics (Noddings, 2002; Sidorkin, 2002). In our chapter on YCP, we briefly touched on other possible areas of youth culture that could also benefit from an YCP approach. It is our sincerest thought that YCP could be used with many aspects of youth culture (i.e. video games, skateboarding, etc.).

However, as our primary experiences have been in the classrooms of urban schools, we will focus our efforts on HHBE. In our classrooms, we have found that hip-hop culture is the dominant culture. As previously mentioned, we agree that hip-hop is not the only culture that many youth relate to, but we feel it is widespread enough to speak to many marginalized youth. With this in mind, we believe that hip-hop culture could be useful in building relationships and expressing care with students. We believe that one should use hip-hop aesthetics and practices in an effort to move toward hip hop based practices and to assist teachers in making stronger connections to students real lived experiences (Hill & Petchauer, 2015).

My dissertation was a case study about a teacher whom used his experiences with hip-hop to foster relationships with and exhibit care for his students. This is relevant because the teacher draws on his own personal experience with hip-hop to push back against a very real generational divide in hip-hop and the larger dismissal of youth and youth culture. The teacher in the case study used his personal experiences to help him relate to his students. John and I found a common thread in this case study with our pedagogical approaches to education. This chapter will give you a brief synopsis of the case study and hopefully convince you to get on board.

A Case Study

The purpose of this case study was to gain an understanding of the teacher-student relationship in an HHBE classroom through the theoretical frameworks of pedagogy of relation and the ethic of care (Noddings, 2002; Noddings, 2007, Sidorkin, 2002). In this research, I studied a middle school classroom to explore teacher-student relationships. This case study focused on experiences in this classroom from the teacher's perspective to gain an understanding of these teacher-student relationships. My primary aim was to find out how the teacher used the ethic of care and pedagogy of relation to build relationships with students. In this case study, the teacher was given a pseudonym of Mr. Wayne. Through interviews, I attempted to gain an understanding of Mr. Wayne's tactics for building relationships in his classroom. Through focus groups with students and observations of the HHBE classroom, I attempted to gain an understanding of student perspectives in this HHBE classroom and how these perspectives relate to the Mr. Wayne's experiences.

The methodology for this study was qualitative and phenomenological. Yin (2009) explains that a case study approach is appropriate for researchers to understand a contemporary phenomenon within its real life context. This aligned with my goal to experience the phenomenon of teacher-student relations in a HHBE classroom. I used three modes of inquiry for this study. They included teacher interviews, focus groups and participant observation.

The findings of this study were relevant to this book because they helped lead to my understanding of using youth culture as pedagogical practice. The major findings included interpretations of how the Mr. Wayne interacted with his class and how he used hip-hop to foster relationships. Findings included Expressed Care, Mutuality, Illustrations, Hip-Hop Mentality and Instructive not Punitive. Through the stated modes of inquiry, each of these themes emerged throughout the study as Mr. Wayne developed relationships with his students. As these relationships were developed, his attention to care was obvious. What I also noticed was how much he embraced and reinforced youth culture as he worked with his students. It was almost like it was woven into his approach to curriculum. I will give a brief synopsis of the findings and then explain what role they play within YCP.

Expressed Care

Expressed care in this case study represents Mr. Wayne's willingness to find things in common with his students and subsequently use a communal attitude in his classroom philosophy. He similarly mentioned that he felt that his commitment to assure that his students did the right thing was a sign of his care. He commented that finding things in common with his students allowed him to break through barriers and allowed for trust to pour into the relationship. He incorporated care with a hip-hop mentality by offering students a chance to be a part of the classroom community. Although, the majority of the students acknowledged they felt cared for, there were some students who did not feel that they were a part of that community. Regardless, Mr. Wayne intently made an effort to make sure that all students understood and acknowledged that he cares for them. Admittedly, even the students in the focus group who did not feel like they were a part of the community still admitted a sense of feeling cared for.

Mr. Wayne employs Noddings (2002) key care components within his classroom using HHBE as his major approach. First, evidence of Noddings (2002) fundamental tenets of ethic of care, primarily that the students are cared for and that they acknowledge that they are cared for, are present within this classroom. Second, the four key components of her philosophy; modeling care in the classroom, allowing for "open-ended … and genuine dialogue", a commitment to producing people who care for others, and the affirmation and encouragement of the best in students are also present within the classroom (Noddings, 2002, p. 23). Mr. Wayne uses HHBE to initiate and facilitate dialogue with his students. Students are also encouraged to perpetuate dialogue with the teacher. He also models care for his students in an effort to convince them to use care themselves with others. He hopes for the best in his students, citing views from HHBE to help tie in social justice themes. The intersection of these key elements poses the conclusive viewpoint that the aesthetics of HHBE retain at least a part of care tenets.

Mutuality

Mutuality is a concept that Sidorkin (2002) argues should be a goal of educators. However, due to an imbalance of power in the teacher-student relationship, true mutuality may be difficult to attain. A key point from Sidorkin's research is that "teachers have very little [control] over students until they create [a] personal relationship with [them]" (Sidorkin, 2002, p. 5). He then suggests that a teacher use a polyphonic authoritative approach in which the teacher transfers power to the students in order to give them a voice. Thus, through polyphonic authority, mutuality is created.

Conclusions garnered from this study determine that a polyphonic approach may be difficult to achieve. Through commonality, feelings of family, community and comfort, Mr. Wayne worked to create a feeling of mutuality. I observed Mr. Wayne seeking a common ground with which to create relationships and I observed him making an effort to depict his classroom as a community. It is important to note that this finding spoke to Mr. Wayne's' ideas of what he has in common with students in order to facilitate relationships and how his students view this commonality. He worked to create a communal atmosphere for his students in the classroom as well as trying to prepare them to be global citizens. He also worked to achieve a sense of family and give his students a sense of family in the classroom. All of these traits led me to conclude that he was working toward a sense of mutuality. However, a sense of full mutuality was unable to be reached in the classroom. One of the causes may be that he was never able to reach true polyphonic authority in the classroom.

Hip-Hop Mentality

While some have used the term hip-hop mentality as a negative precursor to the hip-hop nation (Davey D, n.d.), Mr. Wayne used it as a term of strength and resilience. When we use the term in this book, we mean building from what you already have to create something new. As previously mentioned, making something out of nothing is the very foundation for hip-hop music and culture. In other words, the teacher should use past knowledge of his students and layer this knowledge to form lasting relationships that are based on care. Hip-hop was born out of a need for inner-city youth in the hardest hit socio-economic area of the South Bronx to be creative. This creative energy burned brighter than their impoverished setting and thus they came up with a way to create music with no instruments. DJ's created music by taking two turntables and records and back-to-backing the breakbeat of a song. Mr. Wayne lived by the same principal in his classroom.

His practice also coincides with Petchauer's (2015) HHBE second wave theory since Mr. Wayne samples and layers based upon his relationships, and demonstrated care for his students based upon what he already knew about them. He took the time to get pieces of information about his students as he got to know them. He reused this information to help strengthen his relationship with his students.

Illustrations

Conclusions from the data also revealed that Mr. Wayne shared a collective of examples, analogies, excerpts and vignettes from his life with the students in his class. His use of this collective was consistent and purposeful. I called this entire collective "illustrations" because he painted a picture that made his viewpoint clear and relevant for students. Using illustrations is a means to clarify or demonstrate care to students. Additionally, using illustrations can help sustain relationships. Sidorkin (2000) theorizes that relationships always involve some aspect of emotion, attitude and past history. Evidence of all of these is recognized in the data evolving from this study.

Mr. Wayne's hip-hop mentality fueled the illustrations that he used in his classroom. Illustrations in the classroom are the embodiment of a hip-hop performance for a teacher. When he uses an example or an analogy to help explain an academic concept, Mr. Wayne takes it a step further by connecting the academic concept to something to which the students can relate, thus, creating an avenue for understanding with a thorough explanation. When the students make this connection, it allows them to put their own meaning to his concept and makes the material more relatable to them. In a similar fashion, the excerpts and vignettes connect Mr. Wayne to his students because he is being personal and transparent with his students. This transparency supports authentic and genuine care. In the study, his students noticed this and many mentioned that they felt cared for.

I also observed some side conversations during the study. These were generally carried out during sanctioned free time at the end of class. Some of Mr. Wayne's collective of illustrations were carried out in some of these sanctioned conversations. We termed these side conversations as classroom chatter. And while some may see this classroom chatter as disparaging from instructional time, I argue that these moments of conversation are necessary to build a strong relationship with students. Mr. Wayne often participated in these classroom chatter sessions and shared several of his illustrations with students. I believe that these sessions led to facilitated classroom instruction in the forms of less discipline and informal behavior management. Moreover, these precepts align with Noddings' (2002) ideals of care because of their transparency. Her argument that care is a basic moral tenet coincides with Mr. Wayne's use of illustrations.

Instructive Not Punitive

Another approach that Mr. Wayne used to break down barriers was to have a classroom based on instruction and not behavior. In other words, he thought it important to base his classroom solely on instruction and not base it around the behaviors of his students. This philosophy coincides with Sidorkin's (2002) idea that education is based on relations and not a function of behaviors. During interview sessions, Mr. Wayne explained that his expectations were not set to deal with behavior first, but rather to focus his efforts on instruction. However, during observations, I did observe several instances when Mr. Wayne did speak to students about behavior. For instance, during Mr. Wayne's interview, he specifically mentioned that he would not punish a student who did not have a pencil. On a preceding observation, I witnessed this. However, when the student became antagonistic and refused to accept the pencil, Mr. Wayne, perhaps out of frustration, then punished the student by sending him to the office. While a contradiction from philosophy to one's actions is not uncommon, it must be noted because it speaks to the difficulties of implementing a philosophy such as this.

MC Notes!

"Where's all the hip hop Professors, here to give you more than just text books and lectures, Here to put the pressure on the change and evolution welcome to the re-education revolution, We Moving We Moving."

Get on Board is a shout out to all of the great minds that have laid the foundation in culturally relevant pedagogy, hip-hop based education and the many other ways that describe the various innovative approaches to education today. It is also a call out to encourage educators around the world to "Get on Board" to the mindset of knowing the value of youth culture, not only in school settings, but also in the world. Understand that no child walks into your classroom as an empty vessel with no prior knowledge or experience. They usually come into the classroom with more intelligence than you can see if you are not aware of the power of youth culture.

We are asking you to join us in our sentiment that young people's intelligence being measured by more ways than just their ability to memorize content in which they don't see themselves, yet in which they are expected to excel. Let us gather in support of the students who learn in different styles and need to have the information delivered in different approaches such as Aural, Visual, Kinesthetic, Verbal, etc. We have to understand that we can't continue to have discussions around culturally responsive/relevant pedagogy without putting culture in the driver's seat. All of these discussions and forums must lead with culture to truly ever make sense. Much of the Arts is derived from the culture of Black and Brown people; music, dance, literature and so much more. This is the very reason why we believe all of these cultural sensibilities are the most powerful entry points to our youth around the world. They can see themselves in it immediately.

By ignoring youth culture in both school and the world in general, we are leaving out an entire generation of young people from the conversation. We want you to get on board to these ideas. From my experience in urban school communities, much of the fundamental knowledge that teachers were looking for in their students already existed most of the time. I have also witnessed over and over again these intelligences being discovered through youth culture. The intelligences I am referring to are things like the ability to Freestyle (Rap) or Improvise, Dancing, or even self-expression and many others. My point is that all these things easily connect to school practices as well as life skills across the board when viewed through a YCP lens.

In the chorus of the song "Get on Board", I am calling on all of my Hip Hop Professors around the world who have been "ON BOARD" to continue to challenge the system even further. This movement is growing by the moment because of the collective efforts that are put into this every day. We purposefully made connections with and chose to sprinkle throughout the album some of the hip-hop professors of this day and time. We did this to put some of our people on to these great minds and their amazing work. I am talking about people like Dr. Gloria Ladson-Billings, Dr. Thandi Hicks Harper, Martha Diaz, Dr. Joycelyn Wilson, Dr. Bettina Love, Dr. Chris Emdin, Dr. David E. Kirkland and more. Open your hearts and minds to the reality that if you are a teacher who is teaching a culture that you are unfamiliar with, you are totally missing the brilliance that is right in front of you every day. Until you take the time to study the cultures of your students that you teach every day you will most likely continue to fail to use one of the strongest resources that you have. In other words: GET ON BOARD TO YOUTH CULTURE POWER!

Audi 5000

We want you to get on board! The current system of education in America has several areas that could use some improvement. As we have been discussing, one primary area for improvement that we have observed is the behavioral approach over a relational approach within our schools. We have discussed a youth culture centered approach for classroom management, behavior centered pedagogical approaches, generational gaps, standardized assessments and lesson plan implementation. We believe this approach could be adopted by rookie and veteran teachers alike. The implementation of such an approach would not be easy and would not occur over night. Such ideals must be eased into educational structures. This is the primary reason for us wanting to teach the YCP approach at the pre-service teacher level. A relational approach to teaching may be easily embraced from the start of one's teaching career. However, a teacher with many years of experience could still adapt their pedagogical process in order to use some of these principles. It really depends on you. Are you in it for yourself or for your students?

Interlude 4: How Did You Do That?

How did you do that? This became one of the most popular questions I was asked by teachers and administrators when discussing student relations. I can never forget walking into a middle school in which I was working a few years ago in East New York, Brooklyn. I was greeted by a student I knew very well who was chasing another student all through the building while knocking down chairs, desks, staff, students and whatever else was in his way. I quickly learned that he was chasing the other student because the student threw water on him while at lunch. Although this was not the safest or smartest thing to do, I was able to get in the middle of the students and I could easily see that the student who I knew was very angry. I looked him directly in his eyes and let him know that I genuinely care about him and didn't want to see him get suspended or even worse, expelled. I asked him to please let it go for me, "just do me this favor and try to calm down and let it go." During this moment he looked at me, knocked a piece of paper off the desk and walked away crying. By this time the principal, dean and guidance counselor were all there to witness this and at the same time asked me: How did you do that?

At the time I didn't really know the answer to that question. However, as I gained more experience teaching, it became more and more clear each step of the way. Let me be REALLY CLEAR and say as smooth as it may sound as I re-tell these stories and share my experience, none of this is EASY. I was literally going into school every day failing my way to success and learning from my mistakes and assumptions. I began to realize more and more that it all starts with C.A.R.E. and nothing else even matters if there is no genuine connection with the students. This connection mostly comes from the human element. Young people can tell if you like them or not and if you genuinely care for their well-being. That is where it starts and of course throughout this book and on the album we share various perspectives on how we achieved these student relationships. The reason we decided to call this book Youth Culture Power is because we have been able to witness the dynamic force of youth culture to open new doorways and paths in education.

After plenty of dedication and hard work, some of the most magical experiences I have been a part of in my educator journey has been seeing the innovation work right before my eyes. For example, it was incredible to watch so many students create art (whether it be a drawing, painting, poem, rap, song, skit etc.) around concepts they couldn't grasp before; and now all of a sudden they can think more critically about the content because it was objectified for them through the art. This is only some of the magic that answers this question and I am blessed to embrace the selflessness and passion that comes with being an educator. We are lifelong learners hoping to add on to the conversations and impact that has been going strong in this space. So far, we did it by studying the blueprints from all of those before us laying the path. We give thanks.

References

Davey D's Hip Hop Corner: Where hip hop & politics meet. (n.d.). Retrieved from http://daveyd.com/

[Elon University]. (2012, March 15). Christopher Emdin speaks to Elon teaching fellows [Video File]. Retrieved from https://www.youtube.com/watch?v=a9Ob2CRjh94

Emdin, C. (2016). *For white folks who teach in the hood: And the rest of y'all too.* Boston, MA: Beacon Press.

Hill, M. L. & Petchauer, E. (Eds.) (2015). *Schooling hip-hop: Expanding hip-hop based education across the curriculum.* New York, NY: Teachers College Press.

Ladson-Billings, G. (1995b). Toward a Theory of Culturally Relevant Pedagogy. *American Educational Research Journal, 32*(3), 465–491.

Noddings, N. (2002). *Educating moral people: A caring alternative to character education.* New York, NY. Teachers College Press.

Noddings, N. (2005). *The challenge to care in schools: An alternative approach to education* (2nd ed.). New York, NY: Teachers College Press.

Noddings, N. (2007). *Philosophy of education* (2nd ed.). Cambridge, MA. Westview Press.

Petchauer, E. (2009). Framing and reviewing hip-hop educational research. *Review of Educational Research, 79*(2), 946–978.

Petchauer, E. (2015). Starting with style: Toward a second wave of hip-hop education research and practice. *Urban Education, 50*(1), 78–105.

Seidel, S. (2011). *Hip-hop genius: Remixing high school education.* New York, NY: Rowman & Littlefield Education.

Sidorkin, A. M. (2000). Toward a Pedagogy of Relation. Retrieved from http://digitalcommons.ric.edu/facultypublications/17

Sidorkin, A. M. (2002). *Learning relations: Impure education, deschooled schools, and dialogue with evil.* New York, NY: Peter Lang.

Yin, R. K. (2009). *Case study research: Design and methods (4th ed.).* Thousand Oaks, CA: Sage Publications.

Hip-Hop Education
Innovation, Inspiration, Elevation

Edmund Adjapong and Christopher Emdin, *General Editors*

Hip-Hop Education is a sociopolitical movement that utilizes both online and offline platforms to advance the utility of hip-hop as a theoretical framework and practical approach to teaching and learning. The movement is aimed at disrupting the oppressive structures of schools and schooling for marginalized youth through a reframing of hip-hop in the public sphere, and the advancement of the educative dimensions of the hip-hop culture. Hip-Hop Education's academic roots include, but are not limited to, the fields of education, sociology, anthropology, and cultural studies and it draws its most distinct connections to the field of hip-hop studies; which in many ways, is the stem from which this branch of study has grown and established itself.

The Hip-Hop Education: Innovation, Inspiration, Elevation series will be the first of its kind in educational praxis. It will be composed of books by artists, scholars, teachers, and community participants. The series will publish global authors who are experts in the fields of hip-hop, education, Black studies, Black popular culture, community studies, activism, music, and curriculum. Hip-Hop Education is explicit about its focus on the science and art of teaching and learning. This series argues that hip-hop embodies the awareness, creativity and innovation that are at the core of any true education. Furthermore, its work brings visibility to the powerful yet silenced narratives of achievement and academic ability among the hip-hop generation; reflecting the brilliance, resilience, ingenuity and intellectual ability of those who are embedded in hip-hop culture but also not necessarily academics in the conventional sense.

For additional information about this series or for the submission of manuscripts, please contact:

Peter Lang Publishing, Inc.
Acquisitions Department
29 Broadway, 18th Floor
New York, NY 10006

To order other books in this series, please contact our Customer Service Department:

(800) 770-LANG (within the U.S.)
(212) 647-7706 (outside the U.S.)
(212) 647-7707 FAX

Or browse online by series:

www.peterlang.com